Table Of C

CW01513074

Mastering English and Tennis.

Enhancing Your English and Tennis Skills: Improve Your Grammar, Reading, and Performance.

"Mastering English and Tennis: Elevate Your Grammar, Reading, and Performance" presents a unique approach to personal growth. By emphasizing practical applications, this book aims to motivate and empower readers on their paths to achieving excellence in both language and athletics. Discover your rhythm in language and sport. It is more than merely a guide to teaching English; it invites exploration of the connection between two vibrant fields. For educators and tennis lovers, it provides valuable insights and practical tools to improve language skills and athletic performance both on and off the court. The book's core idea is that sports can act as a powerful context for language learning. This approach highlights that language acquisition can flourish beyond the confines of traditional classrooms, thriving instead in engaging and interactive settings.

Section One: Introduction, Terminology, Reading Skills.

Section Two: Grammar.

Section Three: Tennis Training for Performance (Physical, Mental, Emotional)

Section Four: The Last Serve: A Life and Tennis Lesson. (Short Story)

Section Five: Epilogue: Embrace Your Inner Strength: The Path Forward.

Introduction.

In a time when communication and physical skill are key to success across various aspects of life, becoming proficient in both language and sports is more important than ever. "Mastering English and Tennis: Elevate your Grammar, Reading and Performance" acts as a unique link between two seemingly unrelated areas: language and athletics. This book is not solely for those looking to refine their English; it invites readers to investigate the connection between linguistic accuracy and the strategic skill needed on the tennis court. Language is our primary means of communication; it shapes our views, strengthens our relationships, and creates countless opportunities. Conversely, tennis requires discipline, focus, and strategic thinking. Both pursuits necessitate similar qualities: dedication, patience, and a readiness to learn from both achievements and setbacks. By delving into these two fields, we can achieve a level of personal mastery that breaks through traditional barriers. In writing this book, I aimed to combine my two passions: the beauty of the English language and the exhilarating experience of tennis.

Conversely, tennis requires discipline, focus, and strategic thinking. Both pursuits necessitate similar qualities: dedication, patience, and a readiness to learn from both achievements and setbacks. By delving into these two fields, we can achieve a level of personal mastery that breaks through traditional barriers. In writing this book, I aimed to combine my two passions: the beauty of the English language and the exhilarating experience of tennis.

The connection between these disciplines is clear. A well-crafted sentence can be as striking as a flawlessly executed forehand. Just as a player analyse their opponent, an effective communicator must evaluate their audience, refine their message, and tailor their delivery. This book will guide you through this complex interplay, encouraging growth in both domains at the same time. For many, English serves as a second language, and the challenges may seem overwhelming. Grammar can feel like a demanding task, and reading might turn into a frustrating puzzle. However, it's important to see that mastering English is not a destination but an ongoing journey. It is an investment in your future—enabling you to express your thoughts, share your ideas, and compete globally. The grammar sections will clarify concepts that often perplex even the most enthusiastic learners. With clear explanations and practical exercises, we will build your confidence in writing and speaking. Improving your reading abilities will enhance comprehension and develop critical thinking, skills that are essential on the court and in everyday life.

Tennis, in contrast, instills discipline and strategic thinking. Each serve, volley, and rally demands keen attention to detail and sharp anticipation. Just like mastering English, success in tennis relies on recognizing patterns, accepting constructive feedback, and committing to ongoing improvement. Throughout this book, you will discover practical drills, mental exercises, and performance-enhancing techniques that link language skills with athletic ability. The goal is to make you not just a better player but a more effective communicator. As you start this journey, I encourage you to be receptive to the opportunities at the intersection of language and sport. This book is meant to be interactive; engage fully with the exercises, reflect on your development, and embrace the challenges presented. Whether you are an aspiring linguist striving for fluency in English or a dedicated tennis player aiming for your next tournament victory, you will find worth in these pages.

Remember, mastery is not only about reaching excellence; it is about the learning journey, the victories, the challenges, and ultimately, the empowerment that comes from growth. Join me on this journey of mastering English and tennis. Let's enhance your grammar, improve your reading, and boost your performance, both on the court and in life. The future is ahead—let's grasp it together!

Section One.

Terminology and Reading Skills - Preparation.

"In tennis, as in life, the net can be both an obstacle and an opportunity—a reminder that sometimes, to move forward, we must first overcome the barriers in our path." The Author..

"Every time you step onto the court of life, with every serve and every rally, the terminology you choose echoes the journey you've undertaken." The Author.

Let's begin with some stories, a warm-up for reading skills, and a bit of role play.

Each stroke in tennis has its own specific vocabulary that can aid in teaching new words and phrases. With its rich history and unique terminology, tennis serves as an excellent resource for English learners to expand their vocabulary. The specialized language related to tennis strokes can help learners improve their communication skills while also deepening their enjoyment of the sport. In this story, we will explore the essential terms related to various tennis strokes through the experiences of our main character, Alex. On a sunny Saturday morning at the local tennis club, Alex, an enthusiastic tennis player, arrived early for practice, eager to refine his skills and learn about tennis terminology.

While warming up with stretches, his coach, Max "Ace" Henderson, arrived carrying two rackets. "Good morning, Alex! Are you ready to ace today's practice?" "Absolutely, Coach! I want to learn more about my strokes," Alex responded excitedly. Max smiled and began with the fundamental stroke of tennis: the forehand. "The forehand is when you hit the ball with the front of your racket. It's a crucial stroke, often used to control the pace of a rally." "Can you show me how to do it?" Alex asked. Max demonstrated the correct stance, grip, and follow-through. "Remember, Alex, your body should rotate, and your arm should extend.

Let's practice some back-and-forths." After mastering the forehand, they moved on to the backhand. Max explained, "The backhand is struck with the back of your hand facing the net. You can do it with one hand or two. Let's start with the two-handed backhand." Alex positioned himself correctly, gripping the racket with both hands. As they practiced, Max highlighted the importance of footwork. "Good footwork places you in the best position to hit. Pay attention to your positioning!" Taking a deep breath, Alex concentrated on his movement and executed a solid backhand shot that soared over the net. "Wow, that felt great!" he exclaimed. With newfound confidence, they proceeded to the serve, one of the most critical shots in tennis. Max explained, "The serve starts each point. It involves tossing the ball into the air and hitting it into the opponent's service box. It's all about power and placement."

Alex practiced his serve, trying out different techniques. "What about the volley?" he inquired. "Great question! The volley is a shot made before the ball bounces. It's usually used at the net and requires quick reflexes," Max answered, demonstrating the technique. "Be ready to react—your opponent might hit the ball hard at you!" After a few volleys, Alex felt the thrill of engaging with the ball at the net. "This is so much fun, Coach! I love learning these new strokes!" As practice neared its conclusion, Max called Alex for a final rally. "Now, let's combine everything you've learned. Focus on your forehand, backhand, serve, and volley as we play a match." As they played, Alex felt a sense of accomplishment, applying the vocabulary and techniques he had just learned. They exchanged friendly banter while enjoying a lively game of tennis. By concentrating on tennis terminology and stroke techniques, Alex not only improved his game but also enriched his English vocabulary. Terms like forehand, backhand, serve, and volley became part of his conversations both on and off the court. This learning experience demonstrated how sports can make language learning enjoyable, transforming the journey from the court to the classroom.

Through tennis, ESL students can practice phrases, commands, and key vocabulary in context. For example, terms like "serve," "rally," "break point," and "game point" can seamlessly fit into conversations, helping learners become familiar with sport-specific language while practicing their English skills. Additionally, much of the communication in tennis is non-verbal. Players utilize hand signals to express strategies or intentions, and they often interpret their opponents' body language to predict their next move. This aspect of communication provides an excellent opportunity for ESL learners to engage in meaningful discussions.

Discovering English Communication through Tennis.

Communication plays a vital role not only in daily conversations but also in various activities, such as sports. Tennis, in particular, offers a great chance to develop communication skills and language through engaging scenarios. By linking tennis-related terminology and situations with conversational practices, English as a Second Language (ESL) learners can improve their understanding while enjoying the process. Picture stepping onto a tennis court where the atmosphere is energetic; players are sharing strategies, opponents are signaling to one another, and coaches are offering advice. Each interaction on the court serves as a valuable example for language learners to enhance their conversational abilities.

Activity: Understanding Body Language Objective: Identify non-verbal cues through role-playing.

Match students into pairs, designating one as the player and the other as the coach.

The coach will use non-verbal cues as the player attempts to deduce the intended strategy.

Once they finish guessing, they swap roles. This exercise provides learners with an opportunity to participate in discussions while also helping them recognize the subtle aspects of communication beyond verbal exchanges. Team tennis, like doubles, introduces an additional dimension of communication. In doubles games, teammates need to communicate clearly to align their movements and tactics. Playing in pairs fosters conversations that can enhance their speaking abilities and boost their confidence.

Role-Play Activity: The Doubles Match Goal: Improve conversational skills within a match context. Directions: Create teams of two. Prior to the match, talk about your game plan. Use phrases like "I'll serve," "You take the net," and "Let's switch positions." After rehearsing, apply your strategy during the game. This interactive exercise will help you practice collaboration, listening skills, and expressing ideas clearly. ESL students can also create dialogues using tennis-related terms, either in writing or speaking.

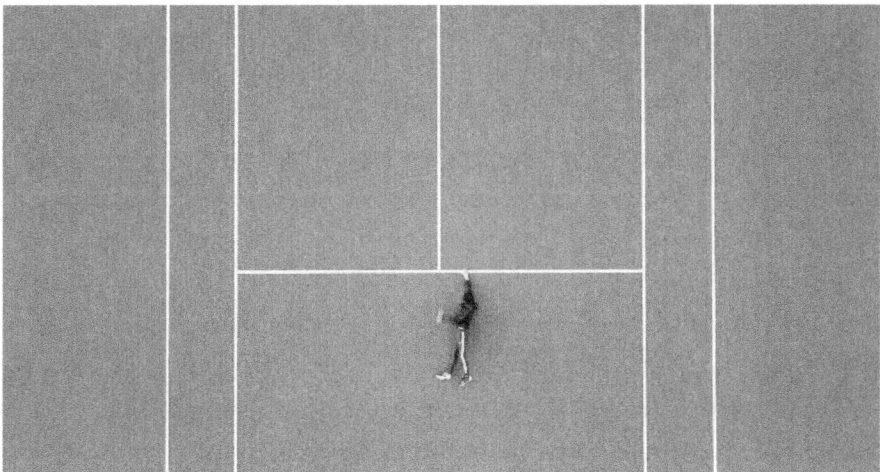

Create a dialogue.

Objective: Use tennis terms in casual writing.

Have students create a brief dialogue between two tennis players as they discuss their upcoming tournament. Encourage them to incorporate various tennis terms, such as practicing serves, analyzing their opponent's strengths, or sharing their preferred playing styles. This exercise fosters creative thinking while allowing students to apply their language skills in context. Using tennis as a theme for communication practice provides ESL learners with an engaging and dynamic experience. Just like athletes on the court, they can enhance their conversational abilities, expand their vocabulary, and recognize the significance of both verbal and non-verbal communication. By closely following tennis-related examples, students can build confidence and prepare for real-life conversations in different social scenarios. Ultimately, whether on the court or in the classroom, communication is the key game that everyone can participate in.

The Power of Teamwork: Tennis Drills and Learning a Language

In the realm of sports, particularly tennis, teamwork might not appear to be a crucial element. Tennis is typically perceived as an individual sport, with players competing solo on the court. Nevertheless, collaborative activities, such as tennis drills, can greatly improve teamwork, communication, and cooperation among players. Likewise, in language learning, particularly in English as a Second Language (ESL) classrooms, group work encourages collaboration and engagement. This story illustrates how the principles of teamwork found in tennis drills can be reflected in ESL classrooms, leading to enriched learning experiences.

At Corden Tennis and English Academy, the ESL program was making a significant impact on students from various countries. The ESL teacher, Ms. Harper, recognized the value of collaboration in acquiring a new language. Drawing inspiration from her own tennis experiences, she decided to integrate group tennis drills into her language teaching approach. The school also had a tennis coach, Mr. Thompson, known for his creative methods in tennis instruction. Ms. Harper viewed this as a unique opportunity and proposed a collaborative project that merged tennis drills with English language learning. On a sunny Tuesday afternoon, students gathered on the tennis court, rackets in hand, while practicing their English vocabulary. Mr. Thompson and Ms. Harper had created a special drill named "Vocabulary Tennis." The students were divided into teams, and each team had to hit the ball back and forth over the net, but with a catch: before each hit, they needed to say a word related to their vocabulary list. The students quickly discovered that verbal communication was just as vital as physical coordination in this exercise. As the tennis balls soared back and forth, laughter and shouts in different languages filled the court.

Each successful hit was met with cheers, enhancing the players' spirits, fostering a sense of belonging, and reinforcing language skills. As the drill continued, students realized they were not only honing their swings but also improving their language abilities through teamwork. Yasmin from Mexico, initially shy about speaking, found encouragement from her teammates. "Can we do this together?" she exclaimed, her voice brimming with excitement after successfully using the word "racket" in a sentence. Meanwhile, in another part of the court, Ali from Syria collaborated with Jenny, a native English speaker.

They seamlessly assisted each other with pronunciation and vocabulary. "Remember to use your follow-through," Mr. Thompson suggested, noticing how teamwork facilitated a natural flow of communication among the students. As the day drew to a close, the students gathered to reflect on their experiences. Ms. Harper led a sharing circle where everyone discussed what they had learned, both in language and teamwork. Ali remarked, "In tennis, I learned to strategize with my partner, just like in group assignments in class." Yasmin added, "Working together made speaking less intimidating for me. I felt supported!" These reflections highlighted that learning a new language involves as much communication and collaboration as it does vocabulary and grammar.

The partnership between Ms. Harper and Mr. Thompson demonstrated that teamwork is a fundamental aspect not only in sports but also in education. By replicating the dynamics of effective tennis drills in the ESL classroom, students could enhance their English skills while embracing the values of cooperation and friendship. This experience revealed the deep connection between physical activities and academic success, encouraging educators everywhere to reconsider their teaching approaches.

Tennis serves as more than just a sport; it is an interactive platform for students to improve their English language abilities. This narrative follows a group of international tennis students who learn the value of reflection sessions following each practice. These sessions not only enhance their game but also solidify vocabulary and encourage spoken language skills. The sun illuminated the local tennis courts as the students gathered for their weekly practice. Among them were Mia from Spain, Sameer from India, and Chen from China, all eager to refine their skills and form new friendships. They circled around their coach, Ms. Thomas, a devoted tennis lover and English teacher. "Today," she said, "after our practice, we will hold a reflection session. This will allow us to discuss what we learned, share our experiences, and practice our English." The students nodded with enthusiasm. Although they had picked up some tennis vocabulary in English, they were eager to apply it in actual conversations.

Reflection Sessions: Enhancing Language Skills Through Tennis.

The whistle blew, marking the beginning of practice. The students spread out across the courts, with Mia concentrating on her serves, Sameer refining his backhand, and Chen honing his footwork. Under Ms. Thomas's attentive supervision, they challenged themselves to improve. "Great job, Mia! Don't forget to follow through with your racket!" Ms. Thomas encouraged, using specific terminology to enhance Mia's comprehension. As they practiced, their bonds strengthened. They cheered for one another and exchanged tips, mixing their native languages with English tennis terms. Laughter filled the air, creating a joyful and educational atmosphere.

Once practice concluded, the students formed a circle on the grass beside the courts, sweaty but smiling. Ms. Thomas invited everyone to share their insights. "Let's begin with what we learned today. Mia?" she prompted. Mia took a moment to compose her thoughts. "I learned how to serve better. I need to add more power," she stated, carefully using the terms they had practiced. "Great vocabulary use, Mia!" Ms. Thomas praised. "Sameer, what about you?" "I improved my backhand," Sameer replied enthusiastically. "But I need to focus on my foot placement." "Excellent!" Chen chimed in, "I learned how to move faster on the court, but I sometimes forget the correct positioning." "Fantastic contributions, everyone!" Ms. Thomas said with a smile. "Now, let's think about how we can communicate these improvements to one another in English." Ms. Thomas encouraged them to ask questions during the session. "Mia, how do you think improving your serve will assist you in a match?" Mia considered, "If I can serve better, I can win more points. It strengthens my game." Sameer then asked, "What drills can we do to work on foot placement?"

As they discussed strategies, Ms. Thomas guided them in using the appropriate vocabulary. They practiced phrases like "footwork drills" and "serve accuracy," enhancing their language skills. By the end of the session, the students had not only worked on their tennis skills but had also broadened their English vocabulary. They talked about terms such as 'baseline,' 'approach shot,' and 'drop shot.' Ms. Thomas emphasized the importance of this for their language growth. "I feel more confident using these words," Chen said, reflecting on how the session impacted his speaking abilities. The reflection sessions became essential to the students' tennis experience.

They reinforced their learning, built their confidence in speaking, and nurtured a sense of community. Through tennis, these students not only evolved as athletes but also as more capable English speakers. As the sun set over the courts, the students left, excited not just about enhancing their skills on the court but also about their advancing proficiency in English. Incorporating reflection sessions into sports can be an effective strategy for language acquisition among students. By fostering an environment where learners can express themselves, reflect on their experiences, and practice vocabulary, educators can significantly enrich their students' lives. Through tennis and conversation, a new realm of communication opened for Mia, Sameer, Chen, and their peers, bridging cultural divides and igniting lifelong friendships.

Enhanced Motivation for Language Learning via Tennis.

Language learning can often feel overwhelming for students, particularly when English is not their native language. Traditional teaching methods may lead to disengagement and diminished motivation. However, incorporating physical activity, especially tennis, into the language learning process can greatly boost students' enthusiasm and help them retain the English language more effectively. This narrative follows a group of learners who revolutionized their English mastery through tennis. On a sunny Monday morning at Corden Tennis and English Academy, Mrs. Johnson, the English teacher, noticed a wave of lethargy in her classroom. A new semester had started, and her students, coming from various backgrounds, were finding it hard to connect with the material. "Alright, class," Mrs. Johnson announced, her voice bringing energy to the room. "Today, we're going to do something different. We'll take our lessons outside and mix in some tennis!" The students looked at each other with confusion.

How could tennis help them with their English? Their skepticism was evident, but Mrs. Johnson continued with enthusiasm, "Through tennis, you will not only learn new vocabulary but also work together. Let's get started!" The transformation began on the tennis courts behind the academy. As the students warmed up, Mrs. Johnson introduced tennis-related vocabulary: "Serve," "Rally," "Deuce," and "Ace." Each term was paired with actions that the students practiced together. "Let's try, 'Can you serve the ball?'" encouraged Mrs. Johnson as students took turns serving to one another. The excitement of the game filled the air, and English began to flow more easily. Laughter erupted as they cheered phrases like, "Nice shot!" and "What a rally!" In this vibrant setting, students experienced a sense of teamwork and competition that helped alleviate their anxiety about speaking in a second language.

Over the weeks, the students showed remarkable improvement in their language skills and confidence. Amir, a once-shy student, now exclaimed, "I can't wait for our next match!" His enthusiasm was contagious, and he often volunteered to be the referee, confidently announcing scores and engaging in light-hearted banter with his classmates. Sarah, a quieter student who had struggled with her English, found her voice by calling out the scores. "One game to me!" she announced proudly, having not only learned the vocabulary but also used it in context during an exciting match.

The combination of movement, language, and social interaction created a deeply resonant learning environment. As the semester unfolded, Mrs. Johnson observed a significant change in the students' language retention and overall engagement. The tennis sessions began to influence classroom discussions, where students used tennis-related language to talk about their lives, communicating entirely in English. During a group project, students collaborated to create a presentation titled "The Language of Tennis." They explored how various tennis terms related to teamwork and effort in learning. Their understanding deepened, demonstrating that their time on the court was about more than just vocabulary; it encouraged teamwork, strategic thinking, and a love for the English language.

By the end of the semester, the students had evolved from hesitant learners into confident English speakers. The integration of tennis into their lessons proved to be an effective strategy for boosting motivation. They were no longer just students in a classroom; they had become a community of learners celebrating each other's successes both on and off the court. The tennis courts turned into a second home, a space where language thrived through play and friendships flourished. As Mrs. Johnson watched them engage joyfully, she realized that the most important lesson was not just about grammar or vocabulary, but about the power of innovative, active learning experiences that enhance motivation through play.

Families were invited to cheer, creating a supportive atmosphere filled with laughter and joy. As the matches unfolded, students shouted words of encouragement and communicated effortlessly on the court. "Watch out for the backhand!" one called, while another shouted, "Let's have a rally!" Each match highlighted not just improved physical skills but also impressive English proficiency. Reflecting on their journey after the tournament, Sarah realized she had ignited more than just a passion for tennis and English. Her students had embraced teamwork, resilience, and the joy of learning. Years later, as her students graduated and moved on, Sarah often thought back to that remarkable tennis class. Together, they bridged the gap between language and movement, forever marking her career with the proof of the power in merging sports and education. In Cebu, the lessons extended far beyond the courts, demonstrating that with a touch of creativity, the world of language can seamlessly intertwine with the joy of physical expression. Often, the most meaningful lessons are learned not solely in classrooms but in the spirit of play. For Sarah and her students, tennis became the catalyst for a lifelong passion for both physical activity and intellectual growth.

Beyond the Game: Confidence and Communication.

Tennis and English: A Perfect Pair for Learning.

In the sunlit city of Cebu, where golden rays shimmer on the blue waters of the Philippines' stunning coastline, lies Corden Tennis and English Academy. Among its most lively figures was Sarah, a kind-hearted and enthusiastic teacher dedicated to helping her students learn English as a second language. Sarah had an innovative idea that would soon connect the realms of physical activity and language learning: tennis. "Why not combine the sport I love with the English language?" she thought one afternoon during her planning session. The concept began to flourish in her mind as she envisioned an engaging and interactive learning experience centered around tennis. The following day, Sarah gathered her eager students at the local tennis academy. Since the academy's opening, she had noticed how the beautifully maintained courts became a hub for young talent.

Students from various backgrounds flocked to the academy, each bringing their unique stories, aspirations, and challenges. With the sun shining brightly, Sarah kicked off her first session with enthusiasm. "Welcome, everyone! Today, we're going to learn not just how to play tennis, but also how to communicate effectively in English while doing it!" As a warm-up, they practiced basic tennis drills while incorporating simple English vocabulary. "Serve," she would say, demonstrating the action. The students would respond, "Serve!" as they swung their rackets.

With each rally, they not only practiced their swings but also improved their pronunciation, absorbing the language through their movements. In the weeks that followed, Sarah introduced engaging tennis-related vocabulary, focusing on terms like "rally," "deuce," and "ace." By linking each term to specific tennis actions, the students improved both their vocabulary and physical coordination. One student, Linh, particularly stood out. A shy girl from Vietnam, Linh discovered a new world in tennis where she could channel her energy. With every swing of the racket, her confidence blossomed. Sarah observed that as Linh became more agile, she also became more inclined to speak up in class, beginning to form sentences with "I think..." As the weeks progressed, Sarah noticed significant development in her class.

The blend of tennis and English instruction created a unique synergy that facilitated cognitive growth. This kinetic learning style allowed students to grasp language in a more comprehensive way. Concepts that once seemed foreign began to feel familiar. The students grew excited about challenging each other in friendly matches. The courts were filled with cheerful banter sprinkled with English phrases. "Nice shot!" would ring out across the nets, while "Great serve!" uplifted each player's spirit. At the term's end, Sarah organized a small tournament for her class. It was designed not only to showcase their emerging tennis skills but also to reinforce their language abilities.

In a world increasingly united by language, effective communication has become essential. For a group of aspiring tennis players in an English as a Second Language (ESL) class, the court transformed from a space for physical training into a lively environment for developing their social and linguistic skills. This is their story of how they enhanced their communication abilities through their love for tennis and friendship. Maria, a dedicated young tennis player from Brazil, enrolled in the ESL tennis program to improve her English while enjoying her favorite sport. However, on her first day, she stood nervously at the court's edge, feeling overwhelmed. "I can hit a ball, but can I express my thoughts?" Maria wondered. Her anxiety arose from the fear of making mistakes in front of her peers. Speaking English felt as intimidating as facing a strong opponent on the court. In the classroom, Maria often felt out of place, struggling to articulate her thoughts. Yet, during tennis drills, she found comfort. Phrases like "Good shot!" and "Let's switch sides!" became her anchors in communication, connecting her with her classmates.

As weeks passed, the emphasis shifted from merely mastering tennis techniques to incorporating social interactions into their practices. Coach Mr. Thompson introduced the idea of "Doubles & Dialogue," where players teamed up to practice their tennis skills alongside their English by discussing strategies, techniques, and personal stories. Maria was paired with Jin, a quiet yet talented player from South Korea. Initially, their conversations were awkward, focusing on basic tennis terms. However, as they played together, they began to share cultural stories, favorite tennis players, and their aspirations. "Maria, what do you love about tennis?" Jin inquired during a water break. "Freedom," she replied. "Each serve gives me a new opportunity. I want to feel that in my English too." Encouraged by their budding friendship, the group decided to enter a local tennis tournament, viewing it as a chance to practice their English skills as well. While training, they created a team motto: "Play Hard, Speak Loud!" This phrase became a symbol of their development—not just as tennis players, but as communicators.

During the tournament, they interacted with other teams, discussing matches, strategies, and sportsmanship. Instead of feeling anxious, each player experienced a growing excitement. Maria found herself cheering, "Let's go!" and "Nice serve!" Each exclamation marked a step toward greater confidence. After their matches, they would review in English, discussing what worked well and what needed improvement in both tennis and communication. On the day of the finals, nerves were high. As they warmed up, Mr. Thompson gathered them for encouragement. "Remember," he said, "you've trained for this moment—both on the court and with your language. Communicate with one another, support each other, and play as a team." With the crowd cheering, Maria and Jin stepped onto the court, filled with determination.

They were no longer just individuals with racquets; they were teammates engaging in dialogue. They communicated in English naturally, intertwining it with their shared passion for tennis. When the final whistle blew, Maria and Jin didn't win the tournament, but they achieved something far more significant—a sense of accomplishment in their ability to communicate. They left the court brimming with confidence, prepared to face interviews, presentations, and everyday conversations in English. Through tennis, they built friendships, gained fluency, and broke down language barriers. The court had evolved into more than just a place for practice; it became a space for growth that extended beyond the game. Their journey highlights a profound truth: when passion meets purpose, social barriers fade, and language becomes a dynamic tool for connection. With their tennis skills and newfound confidence, Maria and her friends now seize every opportunity to communicate, both on and off the court.

Examples of Case Studies and Success Stories.

In the field of tennis coaching, nothing compares to the power of real-life examples that illustrate the successful use of innovative teaching techniques. In this concluding section of Part 1, Chapter One, we will explore testimonials and case studies based on the vast experiences of the author, an experienced tennis coach and language instructor. These narratives not only emphasize his distinctive integrated approach but also showcase the real advantages gained by his students.

The Life-Changing Journey of Sarah.

Context.

Sarah, a 14-year-old aspiring tennis player, came to the Author with a low self-esteem that significantly affected her performance on the court. Having been involved in tennis for only a few years, she struggled with both technical skills and the psychological aspects of competition.

The Author utilized a twofold approach, targeting both her tennis abilities and language understanding. He started by incorporating language activities centered on tennis terms and strategic conversations during their practice sessions. This enabled Sarah to enhance her vocabulary while also connecting more profoundly with the sport.

Over the course of six months, Sarah's confidence soared. She went from being hesitant and passive on the court to taking commanding positions during matches. Her understanding of the game improved dramatically, enabling her to communicate better with her coach and peers, ultimately leading her to win a regional tournament.

Alex's Path to Success.

Context.

Alex was a remarkably skilled junior player, but his technical abilities were often diminished by his struggle to cope with pressure in matches. Despite his talent, he frequently fell victim to anxiety, resulting in disappointing performances.

Recognizing that Alex encountered both mental and technical challenges, the Author introduced focus exercises using a bilingual approach. By teaching Alex calming techniques and sports psychology terms in both English and Spanish, he allowed him to articulate his emotions and strategies in stressful situations.

In just a few months, Alex changed his game significantly. He improved his ability to handle anxiety and developed a keen tactical awareness on the court. This newfound mental strength enabled him to win first place at a national competition, demonstrating the effectiveness of the integrated approach.

Maria's Successful Change.

Context.

Maria was deeply passionate about tennis, but language barriers made it difficult for her to communicate effectively with coaches and teammates. Her enthusiasm for the sport was evident, yet she felt isolated without the ability to communicate properly.

The Author introduced Maria to tennis through an interactive language learning experience. He designed activities that combined physical movement with language practice. As they practiced serves and forehands, they incorporated Spanish tennis vocabulary, making her feel more involved and motivated.

Maria thrived with this method. She not only improved her tennis abilities but also greatly enhanced her social connections within the tennis community. She formed friendships and discovered a sense of belonging. In just a year, Maria was participating in local leagues, signifying her evolution from a newcomer to a vital part of her tennis club.

The experiences of Sarah, Alex, and Maria highlight the significant impact of combining language and tennis coaching. The Authors method not only enhances skill acquisition but also builds confidence, encourages communication, and cultivates a sense of community among players. These examples illustrate how creative strategies in sports coaching can lead to deep and lasting change. As shown by these students, the path in tennis goes beyond skill mastery; it encompasses personal development, resilience, and empowerment.

Second Section.

Grammar.

"Just as a tennis player practices their serve to perfect their game, we must practice our language skills daily to ace the challenges of communication."
The Author.

Tennis transcends being merely a sport; it embodies a vibrant exchange between players that encompasses valuable lessons applicable both on the court and in life. By merging the thrill of tennis with the complexities of language, we form a distinctive platform for learning. In tennis, every shot, whether it's a groundstroke or a volley, relies on accuracy, timing, and strategic thought. In the same vein, mastering grammar requires meticulous attention to detail and the flexibility to adjust to various situations. Just as players hone their skills through regular practice and constructive feedback, English learners can improve their abilities through ongoing exercises and practical experiences.

You will discover all the fundamental aspects of grammar in a tennis context, including terms such as adverbs, adjectives, conditionals, and passives, so let the game begin.

Nouns.

We will explore concrete nouns, proper nouns, abstract nouns, collective nouns, possessive nouns, plural nouns, and both countable and uncountable nouns.

Concrete nouns: Can I physically interact with it? Is it tangible? Does it have a physical impact on me? Can I observe its effects in my life?

Time to play ball!

Picture the excitement of a tennis match. The audience cheers as the players exchange shots, each hit representing not only a physical action but also a testament to strategy and accuracy. Similarly, grasping English grammar entails mastering different elements that form the basis for successful communication.

Similar to a game where understanding the rules and strategies is essential, you will also need to become acquainted with the grammar rules and terminology that we will explore together in this eBook.

The Significance of Nouns.

One of the initial concepts we come across in language—and on the tennis court—is nouns. Nouns represent the names of people, places, objects, or concepts. Just as every skilled tennis player relies on a solid foundation in their strokes, every English speaker needs to have a strong understanding of nouns. In this chapter, we will examine various types of nouns with the same dedication we apply to perfecting backhands and serves.

Concrete Nouns.

Concrete nouns are physical items that can be seen, touched, or interacted with in a tangible way.

Tennis Scenario: Consider the tennis ball, racket, and court. These are all tangible nouns. Now, pose the question to yourself:

Is it okay if I touch it?

Is it genuine?

Will it have any physical impact on me?

Is it possible for me to observe its impact on my life?

For our tennis example, the response would certainly be a clear "Yes!"

Proper Nouns.

Proper nouns refer to specific names of individual people, places, or organizations and always start with a capital letter.

In tennis, referring to Roger Federer or the Wimbledon Championships involves the use of proper nouns. Similar to how each player displays their individual style on the court, every proper noun signifies a distinct entity.

Abstract Nouns.

Definition: In contrast to concrete nouns, abstract nouns denote ideas or concepts that cannot be physically touched or observed.

Tennis Context: Consider terms such as "winning," "teamwork," or "resolve." These ideas reflect the motivations and emotions that propel players during matches.

Collective Nouns.

Definition: These nouns denote collections of individuals or items.

In the context of tennis, terms such as "team" and "crowd" are relevant. Similar to how a coach guides a team of players, recognizing collective nouns enables you to understand language in terms of groups or ideas.

Possessive Nouns.

Definition: These nouns indicate possession.

Tennis Context: Examples include "the racket of the player" or "the trophy of the tournament." Possessive nouns clarify relationships, similar to how teamwork functions in doubles matches.

Plural Nouns.

Plural nouns refer to quantities greater than one of something.

In the context of tennis, "balls," "players," and "matches" are all plural nouns that demonstrate a rise in quantity, which is typical in tournaments.

Countable and Uncountable Nouns.

Countable Nouns: These are nouns that can be quantified, like "two balls."

Uncountable Nouns: These are nouns that cannot be counted individually, like "water" or "advice." Imagine the countless ideas, strategies, and techniques that permeate the atmosphere during a match—hard to measure but essential for your comprehension!

Mastering English grammar is much like excelling in tennis; it requires consistent practice and a deep understanding. As you engage with these concepts, picture yourself on the court; the more you practice, the more proficient you become. Keep in mind that every serve and rally enhance your grammatical abilities, just as each repetition on the court sharpens your athletic skills.

Pick up your racket (and your notebook) and let's kick off the games! By intertwining these aspects of grammar in an engaging tennis setting, you'll enhance your English abilities while having a great time.

Let's maintain the momentum both on and off the court—your path to improving your English begins now!

Verbs.

The simplest way to identify a verb is as a 'doing' word or one that describes an action; verbs act like the ball boys of the English language, serving multiple purposes.

Verbs play a crucial role in the English language, and mastering them can greatly improve your proficiency. In the context of tennis, verbs take on a lively quality, conveying action and energy as they illustrate the actions of players, coaches, and ball boys. This section will delve into tennis verbs, highlighting their significance and the different ways they can be identified and utilized.

What is a verb?

A verb is often referred to as an action word. It signifies an action, event, or state of existence. In tennis, verbs are plentiful, showcasing the various activities and movements that occur throughout a match.

Identifying Verbs.

A simple method to identify a verb is to find words that express an action. In tennis, consider the actions that players participate in:

Serve

Rally

Volley

Smash

Return

Ace

Every one of these terms represents a particular action performed in a tennis match, contributing to the vibrancy of the sport.

The Roles of Verbs

In language, verbs have various roles, similar to how ball boys operate on the court. Here is a concise summary of the function's verbs fulfill in tennis stories:

Action Verbs.

These are verbs that depict physical actions. In a match, the players exemplify various action verbs through their movements:

Run: Players sprint to get to the balls during rallies.

Hit: Players hit the ball with their rackets.

Dive: Players dive for challenging shots.

Linking Verbs.

Linking verbs serve to connect the subject with additional details. In tennis commentary, they often describe a player's condition or performance

The player possesses confidence

Looks: "She looks focused."

Helping Verbs.

Helping verbs work with main verbs to create more specific verb phrases. In tennis, they help deliver precise descriptions of actions

"Will serve" emphasizes a promise or action that is intended to take place in the future.

"Has been training" suggests an ongoing action.

Verbs in Action: Examples.

Examples can further clarify the understanding of verbs in the context of tennis.

Serving.

When a player serves the ball, they initiate the point. Serving is more than just a physical action; it also provides a chance to establish the mood for the rally.

Verb in Action: 'She delivers the ball with excellent accuracy.'

Rallying.

At a rally, players hit the ball to each other in a back-and-forth manner. This interaction is essential to the strategy of the game.

They passionately compete, trying to outsmart each other

Scoring.

Achieving points is the primary goal in tennis. The verbs related to scoring highlight the different methods a player can secure a victory:

Ace: A serve that the opponent is unable to hit.

Break: To win a game while the opponent is serving.

He delivers a powerful serve to score!

Verbs serve as the essential players in the English language, fulfilling vital roles in communication, particularly in the realm of tennis. By grasping and using these action words, learners can enhance their English abilities while connecting with the sport.

In tennis, each match unfolds like a story eager to be shared, with verbs driving the narrative forward. Whether you are a player, a spectator, or a student of the game, harnessing the strength of verbs can enrich your experience both on and off the court.

Now, go out there, practice those verbs, and let your passion for tennis improve your English language skills!

Verb Inflection and Pronouns.

In English, verbs represent the actions that indicate what a subject is doing. They vary based on who or what is carrying out the action, referred to as the subject. Each subject, whether it's the ball boy, a player, or a coach, will align with a specific verb form.

As we enter the realm of language, let's explore how verbs change in the first, second, and third person. This knowledge will make your English as smooth as a perfectly executed backhand!

First Person: "I" and "We"

Begin with the first individual. Picture yourself as the ball boy, excitedly anticipating the start of the match.

I hit the ball

In this context, 'serve' is the verb that highlights your role. As a ball boy, it's your duty to ensure the players are provided with everything they require.

Plural: We collect the balls

Let's bring in a friend! You both are collaborating to collect the balls after the match. The verb gather adjusts a bit to reflect that multiple people are participating. Second Person: "You"

Now, let's turn our attention to the second person, making you the center of our lesson.

Singular or plural: "You struck the ball."

Regardless of whether you are addressing a single player or a team, the verb hit stays consistent. This straightforwardness in the verb form enhances direct communication, making it effective in both coaching and match situations.

Third Person: "He," "She," "It," and "They."

Finally, we arrive at the third person. This is the point where the excitement starts to build, as we picture the players on the court!

Singular (he/she): "He hits the ball." / "She participates in the game."

In these instances, the verbs adjust according to the subject in question. When connected to a third person singular subject, serves and plays need an 's' at the end.

They move back and forth

In this case, the third person plural doesn't alter the verb. Rally remains unchanged regardless of whether you're referring to a single player or a team of players

Having explored the way verbs change, let's take some time to put this understanding into practice. Imagine a singles match where you are both the ball boy and an enthusiastic spectator.

While the players are warming up, you could mention:

I arrange the balls

Observe the players closely

She sends the ball over the net

In the thrill of the game, you might also remark on the players' talents

He serves powerfully

They play aggressively.

When you present verbs within the context of tennis, you not only gain knowledge of English grammar but also connect with the sport, enhancing the enjoyment of the learning process

Regular and Irregular Verbs.

We will now concentrate on the key grammatical tools required to master English—regular and irregular verbs. By relating these verbs to the game of tennis, our goal is to both inform you and provide an entertaining and engaging experience that makes learning memorable and effective.

Regular verbs resemble the reliable athlete on the field who uses the same approach each time. They create their past tense and past participle by adding -ed to the base form. For example, take the verb "to play."

Base form: play

Past form: played

Past participle: played

Similar to how a player swings their racket from back to front in a consistent way, regular verbs adhere to a reliable pattern. During a tennis match, you might hear a coach say:

"You played well during the match."

In this sentence, "played" is a regular verb. Notice how the simple addition of -ed transformed "play" into the past tense.

Instances of Regular Verbs in a Tennis Context

Coach

Base form: coach

Past form: coached

Past participle: coached

She coached the junior team last week

Practice

Base form: practice

Past form: practiced

Past participle: practiced

"They practiced for hours to improve their serve."

Rally

Base form: rally

Past form: rallied

Past participle: rallied

"The players rallied to keep the game exciting."

Exploring Irregular Verbs.

Every match is full of surprises, and similarly, the world of verbs has its own irregularities. Irregular verbs don't simply take on an -ed ending; they transform in distinctive ways. These verbs resemble the surprising underdog who catches everyone off guard with an unforeseen win.

Take, for instance, the verb **"to go"**:

Base form: go

Past form: went

Past participle: gone

Imagine a player rapidly moving toward the ball—it's all about speed and agility! Similarly, the past forms of an irregular verb can catch you off guard.

Examples of Irregular Verbs in Tennis Context

Begin

Base form: begin

Past form: began

Past participle: begun

"The tournament began last Saturday."

Hit

Base form: hit

Past form: hit

Past participle: hit

"She hit an incredible backhand during the final."

Serve

Base form: serve

Past form: served

Past participle: served

"They served the ball with impressive power."

Why Understanding These Verbs Matters.

Understanding the difference between regular and irregular verbs is like knowing when to use a forehand smash versus a backhand slice. Each type of verb has its own strengths and applications in your communication toolkit. Knowing how to correctly conjugate verbs helps students convey their thoughts clearly and accurately. It allows them to describe past events with confidence, whether that's recalling a triumphant match or sharing their personal experiences on the court.

As we serve up examples of regular and irregular verbs in this tennis-themed context, remember that learning English can be as fun and dynamic as the game itself. By practicing these verbs in relatable scenarios, you'll find that you not only improve your English skills but also deepen your appreciation for the sport.

Pick up your racket, head to the court, and take on the challenge of mastering your verbs. Just as every match you play, each sentence you create will bring you closer to becoming a fluent English speaker!

Picture yourself on a tennis court, racket ready, with the sun shining down. You can feel the energy in the air; the excitement is infectious. Tennis is more than just a game; it's a vibrant world of action, strategy, and friendship. What better way to improve your English than by engaging in a sport that communicates universally? We will dive into the verb "to be," a key element of the English language, within the lively setting of tennis.

The Verb "To Be":

What is the Verb "To Be"?

The verb "to be" is unique because it describes existence, identity, or states of being. In English, it takes different forms: "I am," "you are," "he is," "she is," "it is," "we are," and "they are." Let's see how these phrases can connect with the world of tennis.

Dialogue: The Match Day

Characters:

Alex: An enthusiastic tennis player learning English.

Sam: Alex's coach, fluent in English, eager to help with the learning process.

Alex: (tying shoelaces) "Sam, I am ready for our practice today! Tennis is my favourite sport."

Sam: "Great to hear, Alex! And you are improving every day. Remember, today we focus on serving!"

Alex: "What is a serve exactly? Is it easy?"

Sam: "Yes, a serve is the first shot in a rally. It is very important because it sets the tone for the point. Are you excited?"

Alex: (smiling) "I am very excited! I want to learn how to win points."

Bringing "To Be" into Practice

Alex grips the racket tightly, eager to put words into action.

Sam: "Let's start with the basics. Your stance is crucial. You are in the right position; now let's practice the serve.

Drop the ball.

Swing your racket.

It is all about timing and power!"

Alex: "I hope my serve is strong enough!"

Sam: "It will be! Just remember, practice makes perfect. You are resilient; you will get there!"

Alex: "What if I miss the serve?"

Sam: "That is okay! Everyone misses sometimes, even professionals. What is important is that you keep trying. The court is where we learn, and every mistake is a chance to improve!"

Exploring More with "To Be"

As they move from serving practice to actual gameplay, the dialogue turns more vibrant, and the use of "to be" becomes even clearer.

Alex: "This feels amazing! I am enjoying this practice a lot!"

Sam: "I am glad to hear that. Remember, we are a team. When you hit the ball, it is not just about power; it is also about accuracy."

Alex: "I see! I want to be as good as you someday!"

Sam: "You will be if you keep this attitude. Let's move to doubles. You are going to love playing with a partner!"

Through the engaging dynamics of tennis, Alex learns not only the critical elements of the game but also deepens his understanding of the English language. By utilizing the verb "to be," they navigate the complexities of both language and sport.

Learning English through tennis is not just about language; it's about connection, fun, and personal growth. So grab your racket, find your passion, and let's hit the court!

Understanding Past Tense Verb Forms

Past Tense Regular Verbs.

As we begin our transition from the court to the classroom, it is important to understand how verbs change when we refer to the past. In this section, we will examine the past tense of verbs, particularly regular verbs—an important element for effectively communicating our experiences on the tennis court.

Regular Verbs in the Past Tense

Regular verbs are straightforward and dependable, adhering to a consistent pattern when transitioning to the past tense. In most cases, you can just append "-ed" to the end of the verb

Example.

Present: play

Past: played

This pattern remains consistent for a wide range of verbs, allowing learners to confidently construct sentences that recount their experiences.

The Exceptions: Verbs Ending in "e"

For verbs that already end with the letter "e," the transformation is even simpler. In this case, we just add a "-d." This small adjustment means there's less to remember, making it easier to describe past actions without stumbling.

Example:

Present: like

Past: liked

Instances in a Tennis Setting.

To enhance the relevance of this lesson, let's place these verbs in context. Picture yourself recounting a story about your latest matches or practices. Using the past tense enables you to convey what happened clearly.

Regular verbs.

Last week, I played several matches with my friends.

I watched a fantastic tennis game on TV.

Verbs ending in "e":

After the match, I hoped to improve my serve.

I baked some cookies for my teammates to enjoy.

Putting It All Together.

Having established how to recognize and utilize regular verbs in the past tense, let's create a more detailed narrative. Picture sharing an exciting day at the tennis court:

Last Saturday, I played tennis with my best friend, Lucy. We arrived at the court early and warmed up by hitting some practice shots. As we worked on our serves, I suddenly felt a wave of excitement. After a few hours of practice, I realized how much we had improved.

Later, we invited some of our other friends to join us for a friendly match. Everyone enjoyed the game immensely. I made some great shots, and Lucy advanced to the next round with her amazing serves. We all laughed and celebrated the day with some snacks afterward.

Understanding how to convey past actions using regular verbs is an essential step in mastering English. As you continue learning, integrating these verbs into your narrative will help paint vivid pictures of your experiences on the tennis court and beyond. Remember, the past tense opens the door to storytelling, allowing you to share your journey from the court to the classroom in engaging ways. The more you practice, the more fluent and confident you will become!

Past Tense Irregular Verbs.

Welcome back to a place where the vibrant world of tennis meets the thrilling adventure of learning English! now we will dive into irregular verbs in the past tense, integrating them into a story that unfolds on the tennis court, turning dull grammar rules into captivating narratives. So, pick up your racket and let's ace some past tense fun!

Match Day Memories.

It was a sunny Saturday morning when Maria went to the tennis club for the championship match. The excitement filled the air, and she knew she had to perform well. Recalling her training, she took a deep breath and felt prepared.

As she joined her teammates, they spoke about their strategies. "We really saw our opponents' weaknesses during the last match," one player said with confidence. Maria remembered how they had practiced tirelessly the previous weeks, hitting the courts every evening until the sun set. This dedication, she thought, made them stronger.

The Game Begins.

When the match started, Maria played with enthusiasm. She hit powerful serves and ran swiftly across the court. Every time she returned the ball, the crowd cheered. But during the first set, her opponent won a few games, and Maria felt the pressure.

"Don't worry, just focus on your game!" her coach told her after the set. With renewed determination, Maria came back for the second set. She knew this was her moment to shine.

A Turning Point.

In the final game, Maria saw an opportunity. Her opponent missed a critical shot, and Maria quickly made her move. She served an ace that gave her an edge. The crowd went wild! It was a defining moment that created a ripple of energy throughout the stadium.

As she looked at her coach, she felt a surge of confidence. "I have done all the right preparations," she thought. This integral belief led her to concentrate on every point thereafter.

Victory and Reflection.

Finally, after a tense final few points, Maria won the match! She jumped in the air, filled with joy. As she walked over to shake hands with her opponent, she realized that all her training had paid off.

Later, when she sat down with her teammates, they celebrated their victory. "Remember when we practiced those tough drills?" one teammate said. "All that hard work really brought us here."

Maria thought back to all their recent matches, how they had fought through their ups and downs. In that moment of victory, she understood a valuable lesson: success comes from perseverance and teamwork.

In our journey of learning English through the lens of tennis, we've navigated not only the past tense irregular verbs but also the essence of teamwork, determination, and celebration. Remember that mastering these verbs, like mastering a perfect serve, takes time and practice! Keep playing, keep learning, and remember, just like in tennis, every point in the past is a step towards your future successes.

Past Tense Irregular Verbs Recap.

Go → Went

Know → Knew

Take → Took

Feel → Felt

Speak → Spoke

See → Saw

Say → Said

Run → Ran

Make → Made

Win → Won

Come → Came

Do → Did

Keep practicing these verbs in your tennis stories, and you'll ace your English just like you ace your serves!

Past Participles.

At the thrilling crossroads of tennis and language, we continue to delve into the captivating realm of English grammar, with a particular emphasis on past participles. Grasping past participles is essential for mastering English, and today we will investigate how these verbs can improve our communication while we enjoy the game of tennis.

What is a Past Participle?

A past participle is a verb form commonly used in perfect tenses and passive constructions. Although it is a crucial grammatical component, it is not considered a tense on its own. Understanding past participles can help language learners establish a more solid foundation in English.

Forming Past Participles: Regular Verbs.

First, let's look at how to form past participles, starting with regular verbs. For regular verbs, the past participle is generally created by adding "-ed" to the base form. Here are a few examples that could be encountered on the tennis court:

Play → Played

Bump → Bumped

Serve → Served

In a tennis context, these forms can be used effectively in various sentences. Consider the following examples:

I have played tennis for five years.

She has served the ball perfectly.

They have bumped into each other on the court.

Using the past participle in perfect tenses helps indicate an action that has happened at some point before now.

Forming Past Participles: Irregular Verbs.

Now, let's turn our attention to irregular verbs. Unlike regular verbs, the past participle forms of irregular verbs do not follow a predictable pattern, which can make them a bit tricky to learn. Here are some essential irregular verbs relevant to tennis:

Go → Gone

Hit → Hit

Take → Taken

Again, in a tennis context, these verbs can be incorporated into sentences like the following:

I have gone to the tournament every year.

He has hit the ball out of bounds.

They have taken lessons at the local club.

Recognizing these irregular forms is essential for effective communication and helps to create a more dynamic description of actions related to tennis.

Practical Exercises to Master Past Participles.

To solidify your understanding of past participles, let's engage in some practical exercises. These will help you practice both regular and irregular past participles in a real tennis context.

Exercise 1: Fill in the Blanks

Complete the following sentences by filling in the blanks with the correct past participle form of the verb in parentheses:

I have __ (try) my best to improve my serve.

She has __ (win) several matches this season.

They have __ (go) to the final tournament.

Exercise 2: Match the Sentences

Match the correct past participle with its base verb:

A. Serve

B. Hit

C. Break

Played

Gone

Broken

Understanding past participles in a tennis setting not only enhances your English vocabulary but also brings the excitement of tennis into your language-learning journey. By practicing these forms and using them within relevant contexts, you will gain confidence in your speaking and writing skills. So, whether you're discussing your performance on the court or describing a thrilling match, you'll have the grammatical tools you need at your disposal.

Embrace the challenge and continue exploring how tennis and language intertwine, enriching both your sporting and linguistic abilities. Happy learning!

Understanding Present Participles.

Learning a new language can sometimes feel like an uphill battle, but what if you could combine the thrill of your favourite sport with the challenge of mastering English? In our journey through "From Court to Classroom," we'll dive into the exciting world of present participles, utilizing the sport of tennis as our engaging backdrop.

Present participles are an essential part of English grammar, reflecting actions that are currently happening. They are formed by taking the base form of a verb and adding -ing to it. In tennis, numerous actions we perform on the court are expressed through present participles, providing a great context to enhance our understanding of this grammatical structure.

What Are Present Participles?

Definition and Usage

In simple terms, a present participle is formed by adding -ing to the base form of a verb. Present participles serve multiple purposes in English, including:

Continuous Tenses: They help form continuous verb tenses to express ongoing actions.

Example: "I am playing tennis."

Adjective Form: Present participles can function as adjectives, modifying a noun.

Example: "The serving player scored an ace."

Gerund Form. They can act as nouns in some sentences.

Example: "Rallying is a crucial skill in tennis."

Understanding how present participles work creates a bridge between language learning and sport, making it easier to grasp while engaging with a passion for tennis.

Exploring Tennis Actions.

Let's take a closer look at some common tennis actions that can be expressed using present participles:

Playing

Playing is perhaps the most fundamental action in tennis. It refers to the act of engaging in the game.

Example Sentence: "I love playing tennis every Saturday."

Serving

Serving is an essential part of starting a point in a match. It sets the tone for the rally that follows.

Example Sentence: "He is serving with incredible speed."

Rallying

Rallying refers to the series of hits back and forth between players. It's an important skill to develop as you grow in the game.

Example Sentence: "They are rallying beautifully, showcasing their skills."

Volleying

Volleying involves striking the ball before it bounces, a crucial technique when approaching the net.

Example Sentence: "She's been volleying effectively during practice."

Hitting

Hitting the ball is a general term that encompasses various strokes in tennis.

Example Sentence: "I enjoy hitting the ball cross-court."

Practicing

Every player knows that practice is key to improvement.

Example Sentence: "He is practicing his forehand to improve his game."

Creating Sentences with Present Participles

Now that we have explored several tennis-related present participles, let's practice forming complete sentences using them. This exercise will not only reinforce your understanding of present participles but also enhance your ability to describe actions and scenarios in tennis.

Rallying

"The players are rallying intensely, demonstrating their competitive spirit."

Serving

"She is serving the ball with precision, aiming for the corners."

Training

"The team is training hard to prepare for the upcoming tournament."

Winning

"He is winning matches with his powerful backhand."

Using the thrilling world of tennis to understand present participles not only makes language learning more engaging but also allows for practical applications of the concepts learned. Through this approach, we not only grasp the rules of English but also enrich our experience and enjoyment of the sport.

We will continue to explore more complex grammar structures and vocabulary related to tennis, proving that learning English can be both fun and fruitful. Grab your racquet, and let's keep the momentum going on this exciting learning journey from court to classroom!

Auxiliary Verbs.

Introduction to Auxiliary Verbs.

In the English language, we often categorize verbs into different types based on their characteristics. Some common categories include regular and irregular verbs, as well as strong and weak verbs. While understanding these categories is important, an equally crucial aspect of English verbs is their use of auxiliary verbs. These auxiliary verbs, or helping verbs, play an essential role in forming various tenses and moods in sentences.

What are Auxiliary Verbs?

The three main auxiliary verbs in English are be, have, and do. These verbs can stand alone in sentences or be combined with other verbs to create different meanings and grammatical structures. In a tennis context, understanding how to use these auxiliary verbs can enhance your communication skills both on and off the court.

The Auxiliary Verb "Be"

The verb "be" is commonly used to indicate the existence or state of someone or something. In tennis, "be" can help describe conditions, actions in progress, or the general state of the game.

Present Simple: "I am a tennis player."

Past Simple: "She was excited after winning the match."

Present Continuous: "They are practicing their serves right now."

Past Participle: "The matches have been intense this season."

The Auxiliary Verb "Have"

The verb "have" is often used to indicate possession and to form perfect tenses. In tennis, "have" can communicate aspects of experience and achievement, as well as the completion of actions.

Present Simple: "I have a new racket."

Past Simple: "He had a great serve last match."

Present Perfect: "We have played three games this week."

Past Perfect: "They had trained hard before the tournament."

The Auxiliary Verb "Do"

The verb "do" serves as a helper for forming questions and negatives. In tennis, it can also emphasize actions or indicate routine behaviours, making it a versatile auxiliary verb.

Present Simple: "Do you train every day?"

Past Simple: "Did she win the last match?"

Negative Form: "I do not like to play in the rain."

Emphasis: "I do enjoy practicing my forehand."

Using Auxiliary Verbs in the Context of Tennis

Auxiliary verbs help create more dynamic sentences and can significantly enrich your language skills, particularly in the context of tennis. To illustrate their usage, here are a few practical examples:

Describing Skills.

"I am learning to improve my backhand."

"He has become one of the best players in the region."

"They do attend training sessions regularly."

Talking About Matches.

"The match is being played under challenging conditions."

"I have watched every match of the tournament so far."

"Did you see how well she played?"

Expressing Future Plans.

"I will be training hard this upcoming week."

"They are going to practice together tomorrow."

"We have plans to join the local tennis club next month."

Mastering auxiliary verbs is vital for anyone looking to improve their English language skills, especially in a vibrant context like tennis. Whether you are discussing matches, training routines, or your favourite players, the verbs "be," "have," and "do" equip you to express your thoughts clearly and accurately. Incorporating these auxiliary verbs into your tennis vocabulary will not only enhance your communication skills but also ensure you engage more effectively with fellow players and fans alike.

By practicing regularly in both on-court and off-court scenarios, you'll find yourself becoming more comfortable with using auxiliary verbs in English, paving the way for more advanced language skills as you continue your journey in tennis and beyond.

Modal Verbs.

Welcome to the next tour in our tennis-themed journey to mastering English! We will explore modal verbs and how they function within the context of a tennis match. Just as each player on a Davis Cup team plays a crucial role, each modal verb has its unique function in the English language. Understanding these verbs will enhance your communication skills both on and off the court.

What Are Modal Verbs?

Modal verbs are auxiliary verbs that express necessity, possibility, permission, or ability. They help us convey different shades of meaning in our sentences. In tennis, just as players adjust their strategies based on the opponent's strengths and weaknesses, we can adjust the meanings of our statements by choosing the right modal verb.

Common Modal Verbs.

The most common modal verbs include:

Can

Could

May

Might

Must

Shall

Should

Will

Would

Let's take a closer look at each of these verbs through tennis-related examples.

The Game Begins: Using "Can"

"Can" is used to express ability or possibility. On the tennis court, players might say:

"I can serve the ball at 120 mph."

"She can return a serve with finesse."

Here, "can" denotes the ability of the players in a match. It conveys confidence and skill, important traits that any tennis player must possess.

Exploring Potential with "Could"

When we use "could," we talk about past abilities or possibilities. This is similar to reminiscing about previous matches:

"I could win the tournament last year."

"He could have played better if he hadn't been injured."

In these sentences, "could" reflects on past ability and hypothetical situations, similar to how players analyze their previous performances to improve.

Seeking Permission with "May"

"May" expresses permission or a more formal possibility. On the tennis court, one might ask:

"May I practice my serve?"

"You may join me for some doubles if you'd like."

Using "may" is akin to showing respect and courtesy among players, emphasizing the importance of communication and protocol in the sport.

The Uncertainty of "Might"

"Might" is often used to indicate a weaker possibility, akin to evaluating strategies:

"I might try a new serve technique in the next set."

"She might hit a backhand down the line."

In tennis, just like in life, outcomes can be uncertain. "Might" effectively captures that anticipation of possible results in a match.

The Necessity of "Must"

"Must" conveys strong necessity or obligation. On the court, this may sound like:

"I must improve my footwork to win matches."

"You must not underestimate your opponent."

In tennis, just as in language, recognizing the need for improvement is pivotal.

Advice with "Should"

When giving advice, we frequently use "should." Consider the following statements:

"You should practice your serve regularly."

"I should focus on my conditioning."

"Should" helps players recognize the best practices and suggestions vital for honing their skills.

Time to Decide with "Shall" and "Will"

"Shall" and "will" are used to express future intentions or promises. On the tennis court, these verbs might be used as follows:

"I shall play my best in the finals."

"I will work on my net game this week."

Both "shall" and "will" emphasize commitment, a crucial trait for athletes aiming to achieve their goals.

The Hypothetical "Would"

Lastly, "would" deals with hypothetical situations, much like strategic planning for a match:

"If I practiced more, I would improve my ranking."

"If they had more support, they would play better."

"Would" gives players a sense of direction to their aspirations, helping them envision their potential future successes.

Understanding and effectively using modal verbs can enhance your English proficiency in the context of tennis and beyond. Just like each player on a Davis Cup team contributes uniquely to the collective performance, modal verbs add depth and precision to our language. Practice utilizing these verbs in your daily conversations, and watch your communication skills grow as swiftly as a tennis ball over the net!

Remember that mastering modal verbs is just another step in your journey. Keep practicing, both on the court and in your conversations, and soon you'll find that your command of English is as strong as your forehand!

Transitive and Intransitive Verbs.

In the realm of learning English, understanding how verbs function is fundamental. One essential distinction is between transitive and intransitive verbs. This differentiation not only helps in grasping sentence structure but also enhances communication skills, especially when paired with engaging themes such as tennis. We will explore transitive and intransitive verbs using tennis as our context, making the learning process both effective and enjoyable.

Before diving into transitive and intransitive verbs, let's review what a verb is again. A verb is a word that expresses an action, occurrence, or state of being. Fundamentally, verbs are the backbone of sentences, and their proper identification is crucial in both writing and speaking.

What Are Transitive Verbs?

Transitive verbs are action verbs that require one or more objects to complete their meaning. In simpler terms, if you can ask "what?" or "whom?" after the verb and get a meaningful answer, then it is likely transitive.

Example in Tennis:

The player hit the ball.

In this sentence, "hit" is a transitive verb. We can ask, "What did the player hit?" The answer is "the ball," which serves as the object of the verb.

What Are Intransitive Verbs?

In contrast, intransitive verbs do not require an object to complete their meaning. These verbs can stand alone and still convey a complete thought.

Example in Tennis:

The player sprinted.

Here, "sprinted" is an intransitive verb. There's no object; the action of the player stands alone, giving a complete thought without needing to specify what was sprinted towards.

Examples of Transitive and Intransitive Verbs in Tennis.

To illustrate the use of transitive and intransitive verbs in the context of tennis, let's look at more examples:

Transitive Verbs:

The coach teaches the players.

She served the ball.

They practiced their swings.

In each of these examples, we can identify clear objects: "the players," "the ball," and "their swings," respectively.

Intransitive Verbs:

The players practice.

He jumped.

They celebrated.

In these sentences, the actions do not require an object to complete their meaning, illustrating the nature of intransitive verbs.

Why This Matters.

Understanding the difference between transitive and intransitive verbs is crucial for effective communication. In tennis, learning specific vocabulary through clear examples can make it easier to absorb these grammatical concepts. This approach not only enriches one's vocabulary but also enhances the ability to construct clear and concise sentences—skills that are invaluable both on and off the court.

Practice Exercises.

To solidify your understanding of transitive and intransitive verbs in a tennis setting, try the following exercises:

Identify the verb and its type (transitive or intransitive) in the following sentences:

The player won the match.

The team celebrated their victory.

He returned the serve.

The crowd cheered.

Create your own sentences using transitive and intransitive verbs related to tennis.

Learning English through the lens of tennis provides an engaging way to recognize and practice transitive and intransitive verbs. By associating language with a sport that many enjoy, learners can deepen their understanding of grammar while also embracing an active and dynamic subject. Keep practicing, and soon, you'll be serving up sentences with the same finesse as a tennis pro!

Verbs That Are Not Verbs.

In our exploration of English verbs, we've touched upon nouns and detailed the functionality of traditional verbs. However, as we delve deeper, we uncover that some words function in a way that might not be immediately recognizable as verbs. This chapter focuses on the sneaky nature of verbs in English, specifically within the context of tennis, where we see that not all verbs behave like verbs. We will cover gerunds, present participles, past participles, and infinitives, showcasing how they fit into the tennis vocabulary.

Understanding Gerunds.

A gerund is the -ing form of a verb that acts as a noun in a sentence. In tennis, actions and skills can be expressed as gerunds, which can enrich your vocabulary in a playful context.

Example:

Playing tennis requires a combination of skill and strategy.

In this sentence, "playing" is not just an action; it is treated as a noun. It refers to the activity as a whole.

Present Participles.

The present participle is also the -ing form of a verb, yet it functions differently. It can form continuous tenses or be used as adjectives. In a tennis context, it often describes ongoing actions.

Example:

She is practicing her serves every afternoon.

Here, "practicing" indicates an ongoing action, reflecting what she is doing in the present.

Past Participles.

Past participles often end in -ed (for regular verbs) or take irregular forms. They primarily play a role in creating perfect tenses or acting as adjectives. In tennis, understanding past participles is crucial for discussing completed actions.

Example.

He has mastered his backhand stroke.

In this instance, "mastered" reflects a completed action, indicating that he has achieved proficiency.

Infinitives.

The infinitive is the base form of a verb, usually preceded by "to." Infinitives can express purpose or intention. In tennis, they can describe an action someone intends to take.

Example:

She wants to improve her serve before the big match.

In this case, "to improve" explains what she aspires to accomplish.

The exploration of verbs that are not traditionally categorized as verbs, such as gerunds, present participles, past participles, and infinitives, reveals the complexity and richness of the English language, particularly in a specific context like tennis. Understanding how these forms work allows learners to communicate more effectively and expressively.

Key Takeaways.

Gerunds act as nouns and can describe activities.

Present participles describe ongoing actions and form continuous tenses.

Past participles indicate completed actions and can also serve as adjectives.

Infinitives denote intention or purpose and can describe future actions.

Now that you've grasped how verbs can behave differently in English, particularly through the lens of tennis, you're well-equipped to articulate various actions and intentions both on and off the court. Keep practicing these forms, and you'll be chatting about your favourite sport in English in no time!

Adjectives and Adverbs.

Welcome to the exciting world of adjectives and adverbs! We will explore how these descriptive words can enhance your English vocabulary, especially in the context of tennis. Just as a well-executed serve can elevate a match, using adjectives and adverbs can elevate your use of the English language!

What Are Adjectives and Adverbs?

Before we dive into the world of tennis terminology, let's define adjectives and adverbs.

Adjectives are words that describe nouns. They tell us more about a person, place, thing, or idea. For example, in the phrase "the fast serve," "fast" is an adjective describing the noun "serve."

Adverbs modify verbs, adjectives, or even other adverbs. They often provide information about how, when, where, or to what extent something happens. For instance, "She serves aggressively" features "aggressively" as an adverb modifying the verb "serves."

Adjectives in Tennis.

In the context of tennis, adjectives can make your descriptions more vivid and engaging. Here are some adjectives commonly used in tennis:

Powerful: A powerful serve can be intimidating for opponents.

Strategic: Players must make strategic decisions during a match.

Agile: An agile player can quickly move around the court.

Challenging: Facing a challenging opponent can test your skills.

Dynamic: The dynamic nature of a tennis match keeps spectators on the edge of their seats.

Examples in Sentences.

The powerful serve caught her opponent off guard.

His strategic approach to the game allowed him to outsmart his rival.

She displayed agile footwork as she chased down the ball.

It was a challenging match that required all of her focus and stamina.

The dynamic rallies showcased the intensity of professional tennis.

Adverbs in Tennis.

Adverbs play an essential role in providing depth to your actions. Here are some common adverbs that can be used in tennis:

Quickly: The player reacted quickly to the unexpected shot.

Frequently: She serves frequently to build pressure.

Aggressively: He played aggressively to take control of the net.

Carefully: The doubles team worked carefully to coordinate their movements.

Eagerly: The fans eagerly cheered for their favourite player.

Examples in Sentences:

The player reacted quickly to the incoming serve.

She practices frequently to improve her skills.

He plays aggressively to dominate his opponents.

The team moved carefully around the court during the doubles match.

Fans eagerly awaited the start of the final match.

Combining Adjectives and Adverbs.

Now let's see how you can combine adjectives and adverbs to create richer and more detailed descriptions.

The powerful serve was hit quickly over the net.

She responded to the challenging shot aggressively.

His dynamic playing style allowed him to move easily around the court.

The match started at a frantic pace, with both players moving strategically.

The fans applauded the exceptional rally enthusiastically.

Practice Exercise.

To really solidify your understanding, try the following exercise:

Fill in the blanks with the perfect adjective or adverb.

a. The player hit the ball __. (adverb)

b. The match was extremely ____. (adjective)

c. She always serves ___ during practice. (adverb)

By using adjectives and adverbs effectively, you can describe not just tennis matches but also any action or emotion more vividly. Whether you're discussing a thrilling point or a powerful serve, remember that these descriptive words can make your language more colourful and engaging. Keep practicing, and soon you'll express yourself confidently both on and off the court!

Feel free to use this content as a foundational chapter in your eBook, adapting it as needed to fit your style and vision!

Comparative and Superlative Adjectives.

Welcome to a thrilling journey where we combine the excitement of tennis with the beauty of the English language! In this chapter, we'll dive into comparative and superlative adjectives, helping you express differences and extremes in a fun and engaging way—all within the context of tennis.

Understanding Adjectives.

Before we get into the comparative and superlative forms, let's review again what adjectives are. Adjectives are words that describe nouns. For example:

Fast: The ball was fast.

High: She hit a high shot.

Comparative Adjectives.

Comparative adjectives are used to compare two nouns. In English, we generally form the comparative by adding "-er" to the adjective or using "more" before the adjective for longer adjectives.

Examples in Tennis Context

Fast → Faster

Maria's serve is faster than Anna's two-handed backhand.

Tall → Taller

Mark is taller than Tom, which gives him an advantage at the net.

Strong → Stronger

John is stronger than his opponent, allowing him to deliver powerful groundstrokes.

Exciting → More Exciting

The final match was more exciting than the semi-finals.

Superlative Adjectives.

Superlative adjectives denote the highest degree of a quality among three or more nouns. These adjectives are often formed by adding "-est" or using "most" before the adjective.

Examples in Tennis Context.

Fast → Fastest

Roger has one of the fastest serves in the history of tennis.

Tall → Tallest

At 6'10", Ivo Karlović is the tallest player on the ATP tour.

Strong → Strongest

She is the strongest player in her club, dominating the court.

Exciting → Most Exciting

The Wimbledon finals is considered the most exciting event of the year.

Using Comparatives and Superlatives in Sentences.

Let's see how these adjectives can enhance your sentence structures in tennis discussions.

Comparatives.

This year's tournament is hotter than last year's.

His backhand is better than most players in his category.

Superlatives.

She has the best technique among young players in her region.

This is the most challenging court I have ever played on.

Practice Makes Perfect.

Now that you're familiar with comparative and superlative adjectives, it's time to practice! Here are a few exercises to solidify your understanding:

Fill in the Blanks:

This player is __ (quick) compared to others in the league.

She is considered the __ (talented) athlete of the academy.

Create Sentences:

Use "tall" in a comparative sentence.

Describe your favorite player using a superlative.

Tennis Trivia.

Who is the ____ (famous) tennis player in history?

Which tournament is the ____ (prestigious) in the world?

By integrating comparative and superlative adjectives into your tennis vocabulary, you'll be better equipped to express opinions, describe nuances, and make comparisons that enhance your discussions about the sport. Remember, just as in tennis, practice is essential. Keep using these grammatical tools to refine your English skills and enjoy every moment on and off the court!

Happy learning, and see you on the court!

Other parts of speech in a tennis setting

We have covered a lot of different grammar topics, so what else is left to learn? These are things like phrasal verbs, another type is prepositions, little words like , in , out and by. We will also take a look at articles and determiner words like a, an, the, these and those. We also learn about conjunctions that act as the glue to the English language. Finally we will cover reported speech and the passive voice,

Other Parts of Speech.

As we have journeyed through various grammar topics in our exploration of tennis and English, you might be wondering what else there is left to learn. The world of language is rich and diverse, offering plenty of opportunities to enhance your understanding. Now we will delve into further various aspects of English grammar that are particularly relevant to tennis. These include phrasal verbs, prepositions, articles, conjunctions, reported speech, and the passive voice. Let's get started!

Phrasal Verbs.

Phrasal verbs are an essential part of conversational English, often adding a degree of nuance and specificity that single-word verbs cannot achieve. In a tennis context, you might come across phrases like:

"Serve up": To present something, often used when talking about serving the ball.

"Run down": To chase after a ball that is far away or difficult to reach.

"Hit back": To respond to an opponent's shot effectively.

These expressions can be particularly useful in describing actions on the court in a way that feels relatable and vibrant.

Prepositions.

Prepositions are small but mighty words that help establish the relationship between other words in a sentence. Understanding their usage in a tennis setting can improve your fluency. Here are some examples:

"In": For example, "The ball is in the court."

"Out": "The ball went out of bounds."

"By": "He won the match by two sets to one."

Each of these prepositions provides context that enhances comprehension of player actions and match scenarios.

Articles and Determiners.

Articles and determiners like "a," "an," "the," "these," and "those" help specify nouns. In tennis, these words can help clarify your statements:

"A serve": Referring to any serve in general.

"The ball": Talking about a specific ball you both know.

"These players": Referring to players currently on the court.

Understanding when and how to use these words can significantly improve your clarity when communicating about tennis.

Conjunctions.

Conjunctions act as the glue of the English language, connecting words, phrases, or clauses. In tennis discussions, you might employ them as follows:

"And": "She has a powerful serve, and he has excellent footwork."

"But": "He plays aggressively, but she prefers a defensive strategy."

"Or": "Do you want to practice forehands or backhands?"

Using conjunctions effectively allows for smoother and more cohesive sentences.

Reported Speech.

Reported speech is used to convey what someone else has said without quoting them directly. This can be particularly useful in discussions about tactics or strategies in tennis matches:

Direct speech: "I need to practice my serve," she said.

Reported speech: She said that she needed to practice her serve.

Understanding how to manipulate reported speech enhances your communication skills, especially when relaying advice or strategies.

The Passive Voice.

The passive voice emphasizes the action and the receiver, often at the expense of the doer. In tennis, this structure can sometimes highlight the result over the player:

Active voice: "The player won the match."

Passive voice: "The match was won by the player."

Learning to recognize and use the passive voice can diversify your expressive capabilities, particularly in tactical discussions.

We have expanded our linguistic toolkit by exploring phrasal verbs, prepositions, articles, conjunctions, reported speech, and the passive voice, all within the context of tennis. By incorporating these components into your English practice, you will not only enhance your grammar skills but also improve your ability to communicate during matches and training sessions. Use this knowledge to further enrich your experience both on and off the court as you engage in the beautiful game of tennis!

Now you're well-equipped to tackle these additional grammar elements as you continue your journey through the intersection of tennis and English language learning!

Present, Past, and Future Tenses.

In this section of the eBook, we will explore how to use the present, past, and future tenses in English, all through the lens of tennis. By connecting language learning with the sport, we will make the experience enjoyable and relatable.

Understanding Tenses.

Before we dive into the fun activities, let's review how each tense is structured and how they function in the context of tennis.

Present Simple.

The present simple tense is used to describe habits, general truths, and repeated actions. In tennis, it can describe what players typically do or what happens in a match.

Structure.

Affirmative: Subject + base form of the verb (+s/es for third person singular)

Negative: Subject + do/does + not + base form of the verb

Question: Do/Does + subject + base form of the verb?

Examples.

Affirmative: "I play tennis on weekends."

Negative: "He does not play matches during the week."

Question: "Do they practice every day?"

The use of a timeline can help you visualize the ongoing nature of the present simple tense. Here, you might show a line indicating repeated activities (like playing tennis every weekend) without specifying an exact time.

Fun Activities for the Present Simple.

Tennis Routine Presentation.

Create a short presentation about your routine, using the present simple. Describe your favorite tennis drills, practice schedule, experiences playing matches. This exercise will reinforce the use of the present tense through a familiar context.

Role Play.

Set up a scenario where students simulate a tennis match or practice. One student can be the coach, giving commands or feedback using the present simple, such as, "You serve the ball," or "She runs to the net."

Tennis Vocabulary Bingo.

Create a bingo card containing tennis-related verbs. Call out the verbs in their base form (like "serve," "hit," "practice"), and students can use the present simple to form sentences when they get bingo. For example, if they have the verb "serve," they would say, "I serve the ball."

Moving to the Past Tense.

Once students have a solid understanding of the present simple, we can move to the past tense. This tense allows us to discuss actions that have already occurred, which is essential in tennis when recounting a match or a memorable experience.

Past Simple.

The past simple tense refers to actions that were completed in the past.

Structure:

Affirmative: Subject + past form of the verb

Negative: Subject + did not + base form of the verb

Question: Did + subject + base form of the verb?

Examples:

Affirmative: "I played a great match yesterday."

Negative: "He did not win the tournament last year."

Question: "Did they practice together last week?"

Engaging Activities for the Past Simple

Match Reports.

After a tennis session, students can write a brief report about the match or the practice. I encourage you to use the past simple to describe what happened, important plays, and their feelings about the outcome.

Group Storytelling.

In groups, create a story about a fictional tennis tournament. Each student takes turns adding a sentence using the past simple. For example, "First, I arrived at the court," followed by "Then, I met my opponents."

Looking Ahead: Future Tenses.

Finally, we will discuss the future tenses, which will allow students to express actions that will happen in tennis.

Future Simple.

The future simple tense is used to describe actions that will take place.

Structure.

Affirmative: Subject + will + base form of the verb

Negative: Subject + will not + base form of the verb

Question: Will + subject + base form of the verb?

Examples:

Affirmative: "I will practice every day next week."

Negative: "She will not attend the match tomorrow."

Question: "Will they join us for practice?"

Activities for the Future Simple

Future Training Plans.

Create a detailed training plan for the next month, using the future simple to describe the goals they want to achieve. For instance, they might say, "I will improve my serve," or "We will work on doubles strategies."

Vision Board.

Students create a vision board with images and phrases about their future in tennis. They will use the future simple to describe their aspirations, like "I will compete in tournaments" or "I will become a better player."

By integrating tennis with English language learning, you can grasp the concepts of present, past, and future tenses in an engaging way. Through structured activities and real-life application, they will not only learn grammar but also enjoy the sport you love. Let's take our lessons from the court to the classroom, strike a balance between fun and education, and watch our skills—both in tennis and language—grow!

Understanding the Present Simple.

The Present Simple tense is used to describe actions that are habitual or routine. This includes things we do regularly or facts that are always true. In the world of tennis, this could include actions or routines associated with playing the game.

Structure of the Present Simple.

The structure of the Present Simple is straightforward. For most verbs, you simply use the base form. Here's a quick overview:

Affirmative form: Subject + base form of the verb (add "s" for he, she, it)

Example: Sophia plays tennis every weekend.

Negative form: Subject + do/does not + base form of the verb

Example: John does not play tennis on weekdays.

Interrogative form: Do/Does + subject + base form of the verb?

Example: Does Maria play tennis every day?

Examples.

Affirmative Sentences.

Sofia plays in the park every day.

Marcus practices his serves in the morning.

The coach teaches new skills every Tuesday.

Negative Sentences.

Sofia does not play tennis on Sundays.

Marcus does not practice late at night.

The coach does not teach on holidays.

Interrogative Sentences

Does Sofia play in competitions?

Does Marcus practice every day?

Does the coach give private lessons?

Using Habits and Routines in Tennis.

Understanding how to use the Present Simple tense can help you communicate effectively about tennis. Let's take a look at some common tennis-related phrases and how they describe habits or routines.

Daily Routines.

I wake up early to practice my serves.

I eat a healthy breakfast before I go to the court.

Weekly Rules.

I play doubles with my friends every Friday.

I have a lesson with my coach every Saturday morning.

Game Day Rituals.

I always wear my lucky tennis shoes during matches.

I usually listen to music to pump myself up before a game.

Practice Makes Perfect.

To reinforce your understanding of the Present Simple, practicing with the context of tennis can be both fun and effective. Here are some exercises you can try:

Exercise 1: Fill in the Blanks.

Complete the sentences with the correct form of the verb in the Present Simple.

I ___ (play) tennis every day.

He ___ (not/play) on weekends.

They ___ (practice) every Tuesday.

Exercise 2: Create Your Own Sentences.

Now, think about your own tennis routine. Write three sentences in the Present Simple. Make sure to include an affirmative, a negative, and an interrogative sentence. For example:

I _____.

I do not _____.

Do I _____?

The Present Simple tense is a vital part of everyday communication, especially when discussing routines and habits. By using tennis as a fun context for learning, you'll not only improve your English but also enjoy the game that brings so many people together.

Remember, practice is key! So grab your racket, hit the court, and don't forget to practice your Present Simple sentences. Happy learning and playing!

I hope you're enjoying your journey mastering English and Tennis.

Present Continuous.

In the world of tennis, understanding the present continuous tense can significantly enhance how we describe ongoing actions and temporary situations. This verb tense is used to illustrate actions that are happening right now or are currently in progress. By using the present continuous, we can vividly bring to life the dynamic and energetic environment of a tennis match or practice session.

Understanding the Present Continuous.

The present continuous tense consists of the verb "to be" (am, is, are) followed by the base form of a verb with an -ing ending. For instance, "Maria is walking" or "They are practicing." This structure allows us to convey that an action is in progress at the moment of speaking.

Let's explore this concept in action through a series of scenarios set on a tennis court.

Scenario 1: Practice Drills.

At the tennis club today, the atmosphere is buzzing with activity.

Maria is practicing her serves. She is focused on improving her accuracy and speed. Every time she steps up to the baseline, she takes a deep breath and swings her racket.

Mark is hitting the ball against the wall. He is working on his backhand and trying to increase his consistency. The rhythm of the ball resonates throughout the court as he concentrates on his technique.

Emily and Jake are playing a doubles match against each other. They are laughing and strategizing as they move around the court. The competitive yet friendly banter adds to the mix of sounds on the court.

In this scenario, the present continuous illustrates the various activities taking place during a practice session, emphasizing that these actions are dynamic and ongoing.

Scenario 2: A Tournament Match.

As the sun shines brightly over the tournament grounds, the excitement is palpable.

The players are warming up on the court. They are stretching and hitting practice shots to get into the rhythm before their matches begin. The sound of rackets striking the ball fills the air as they get acclimated.

The crowd is gathering to watch the matches. Fans are chatting, taking photos, and finding their seats, creating a lively atmosphere.

The referee is reviewing the player rosters. She is ensuring all details are correct before the matches commence. Every detail matters in making sure the tournament runs smoothly.

Here, the present continuous allows us to capture the suspense and energy of a live event, painting a picture of what is happening in real time.

Scenario 3: Off-Court Activities.

The life of a tennis player goes beyond just hitting the ball on the court.

Maria is studying her opponent's previous matches. She is analyzing their playing style to prepare a strategy. This preparation is a crucial part of any competitive athlete's routine.

Mark is signing autographs for fans. He is sharing smiles and engaging with the audience after a match, understanding the importance of connecting with his supporters.

Emily is participating in a press conference. She is discussing her journey in the tournament and the challenges she faces. This moment allows her to share her experience and inspire others.

In this context, the present continuous illustrates the diverse aspects of being a tennis player, highlighting activities beyond the court and underlining the dedication involved in the sport.

The present continuous tense serves as an effective tool in the context of tennis. It allows us to vividly express actions and events that are currently in progress. Whether on the practice court, during a tournament, or off-court activities, employing this tense adds depth and immediacy to our descriptions. By mastering the present continuous, tennis enthusiasts can enhance their commentary, storytelling, and overall communication within the sport.

Past Simple.

Understanding the Past Simple.

The past simple tense is used to talk about actions that were completed at a specific time in the past. It is formed by using the base form of the verb plus -ed for regular verbs, while irregular verbs require unique past forms.

Example of Regular Verbs.

Play becomes played

Learn becomes learned

Example of Irregular Verbs

Go becomes went

Have becomes had

Structure of the Past Simple.

The past simple is structured as follows:

Affirmative Sentences: Subject + past verb

Negative Sentences: Subject + did not + base form of the verb

Interrogative Sentences: Did + subject + base form of the verb?

Tennis Stories in the Past Simple.

Let's step onto the court and put our understanding of the past simple tense into practice with some stories!

Emma's Day at the Court.

Yesterday afternoon, Emma played tennis with her friends. She arrived at the court at two o'clock. Emma trained hard for an upcoming match. She hit the ball with power and control. After her practice session, she felt proud of her improvements.

Emma watched a professional match after her training. The players served the ball with incredible speed. She was amazed by their skills. Emma learned new strategies that she could use in her next match.

Mark's First Tennis Lesson.

Last week, Mark decided to take tennis lessons. He found a local tennis club and enrolled in a beginner class. On his first day, Mark met his coach, who explained the basic rules of the game. He started with simple drills.

Mark practiced his forehand and backhand strokes. He struggled at first, but with each lesson, he improved significantly. By the end of the month, he participated in his first mini-tournament. It was a thrilling experience for him!

Sarah's Competitive Match.

Last Saturday, Sarah competed in a local tournament. She woke up early and prepared for her match. Sarah reviewed her strategies and visualized her victory on the court.

During the match, she faced a tough opponent. Sarah served strong and returned every ball. Despite some challenges, she remained focused and played her best game. To her delight, Sarah won the match! That day marked a significant achievement in her tennis career.

Practicing the Past Simple.

Now it's your turn! Think about a past experience related to tennis and write about it using the past simple structure. Here are a few prompts to get started:

Describe your first time playing tennis.

Share a memorable match you watched.

Remember a day at the tennis court with friends or family.

Example Answers.

I played tennis for the first time last summer at a friend's house.

I watched a thrilling match on television last week.

Last weekend, I went to the court with my family, and we had a lot of fun.

Understanding the past simple tense is vital to recounting your experiences. Through tennis stories, you've explored how to use this tense effectively while enjoying the sport you love. Keep practicing, and soon you'll be telling your own tennis stories in English with confidence!

Past Continuous.

The past continuous is a verb tense used to describe actions that were ongoing in the past. It is formed using the verb "to be" (was/were) + the present participle (the -ing form of the verb). This tense can be particularly useful to set the scene in storytelling or when discussing events that were occurring over a period of time.

Understanding the Past Continuous.

Before we dive into tennis-related examples, let's take a moment to look at how the past continuous is structured:

Affirmative: Subject + was/were + verb (-ing)

Example: She was practicing her serve.

Negative: Subject + was/were + not + verb (-ing)

Example: They were not watching the match.

Interrogative: Was/Were + subject + verb (-ing)?

Example: Were you enjoying the game?

Usage in a Tennis Context.

Now, let's examine how we can use the past continuous tense to describe actions that were taking place on the tennis court.

Setting the Scene.

Imagine a bustling tennis academy on a sunny Saturday afternoon. Players of all ages are engaged in various activities as they prepare for their matches. Here are some examples of sentences in the past continuous tense to illustrate this scenario:

Practice Sessions.

The junior players were practicing their forehands while the coaches were giving instructions from the sidelines.

Tournaments.

Last weekend, the local tournament was taking place, and many spectators were cheering for their favorite players.

Injuries.

While Clara was playing a singles match, she was feeling a sharp pain in her ankle, prompting her to call for a timeout.

Attention to Detail.

The past continuous is particularly effective when we want to paint a vivid picture of ongoing actions in the past. This can also be applied to storytelling, where the context of tennis can enhance the narrative. Let's look at a mini-story that utilizes the past continuous:

Micro-Story Example.

On a sunny afternoon, the annual community tennis tournament was in full swing. Players of varying skill levels were competing intensely, showcasing their abilities on the court. As the matches continued, the crowd was filled with excitement. In the midst of a crucial final set, Sophia was serving when she noticed one of her teammates struggling in a nearby match. While focusing on her serve, her mind wandered to how she could assist. Suddenly, she heard the referee announce a score from another game, and she realized time was slipping away.

She contemplated how to adjust her strategy. As she served, her opponent stood ready to return the ball. Spectators around her were eagerly absorbing every moment. The atmosphere was electric, charged with competitive spirit. Meanwhile, a group of children played on a smaller court, practicing their volleys and laughing as they chased after balls. The scene beautifully blended determination and joy, representing the game they all cherished. This exploration of the past continuous tense through the lens of tennis has provided many examples and a context for effective use of this grammatical form.

Whether narrating a match, discussing practice sessions, or sharing personal experiences on the court, the past continuous vividly portrays ongoing actions. Understanding this tense is essential for storytelling and sharing experiences in English. By incorporating tennis-related scenarios, we can make learning this tense enjoyable and meaningful. Next time you step onto the court or watch a match, consider using the past continuous to reflect on your experiences. Happy studying, and may your English journey be as fulfilling as an exciting tennis match!

The Present Perfect Simple.

The present perfect simple is an intriguing tense that links past actions to the present. Unlike the simple past, which indicates actions completed at a specific moment in the past, the present perfect emphasizes experiences, changes, or circumstances that are significant to the current time. For numerous English learners, particularly those who are enthusiastic about sports such as tennis, mastering this tense can be a fulfilling challenge.

Forming the Present Perfect Simple.

The structure of the present perfect is straightforward: it consists of the auxiliary verb "have" (or "has" for third-person singular) followed by the past participle of the main verb. For example:

I have played tennis.

She has practiced her serve.

When we apply this structure to a tennis context, we can better illustrate how to use the present perfect simple.

Examples in a Tennis Setting.

Anfisa's Recent Activities

Anfisa has walked to the court in the last week.

This sentence highlights Anfisa's experience of walking to the court recently, showing that the action has occurred but not specifying when.

Practice Sessions.

We have practiced our serves every day this month.

Here, the focus is on the continuity of practice, emphasizing that the action is not confined to one moment but has ongoing significance in preparing for future matches.

Tournaments Participated.

He has participated in three tournaments this year.

This statement underlines the achievements of the player, reinforcing the importance of these past experiences in their current journey as a tennis player.

Engaging Students with Tennis-Related Activities.

One effective way to help students master the present perfect simple is to incorporate tennis-related activities that require them to use the tense. Here are some engaging exercises:

1. Tennis Timeline Activity.

Ask students to create a timeline of their tennis experiences using the present perfect simple. They can include actions like:

"I have won a match."

"I have learned to serve."

2. Interview a Classmate

Pair students and have them interview each other about their tennis experiences. They should use the present perfect to formulate their questions and answers, such as:

"What skills have you mastered?"

"How many hours have you spent practicing this month?"

3. Group Discussion.

Organize a group discussion where students share what they have done to improve their tennis game. Prompt them with questions like:

"What techniques have you tried to enhance your performance on the court?"

"Have you ever trained with a coach?"

Practical Usage in Communication.

Encouraging students to communicate their tennis experiences using the present perfect simple will not only deepen their understanding of the tense but also enable them to express themselves in engaging ways. For instance, they might say:

"I have met many great players at different clubs."

This sentence not only reveals an experience but also fosters a sense of connection among players.

By blending tennis with language learning, the present perfect simple transforms from a daunting grammatical structure into an accessible and relatable tool. Students can explore their own experiences while practicing English in an enjoyable environment. As they walk onto the court and into the classroom, they bring their past actions to life, fostering both their tennis skills and language proficiency. With consistent practice and creative engagement, mastering the present perfect simple will become an achievable goal for every tennis enthusiast.

Present Perfect Continuous.

You will be sensing a pattern so far, as we are now covering the present perfect continuous. The present perfect continuous is something that is happening in the present, either within a duration or with a sense of recency. For example: Serena has been walking to the court for 10 minutes: Serena has been walking to the park often lately.

The Present Perfect Continuous Tense.

The present perfect continuous tense is essential for understanding actions that started in the past and continue into the present. In the context of tennis, this tense can help you describe ongoing actions that relate to your training, matches, or practice routines.

What is the Present Perfect Continuous?

The present perfect continuous is formed using the auxiliary verbs "has" or "have," followed by "been," and the present participle of the verb (the -ing form). It conveys a sense of duration or recent activity.

For example.

Serena has been practicing her serve for three hours.

Roger has been training daily to improve his stamina.

In both sentences, we can see that the actions began in the past and are relevant to the present.

Practical Examples in a Tennis Setting.

To fully grasp the present perfect continuous, let's dive into some practical examples that bring this grammar point to life on the tennis court:

Training Sessions.

Maria has been working on her footwork for the last month.

This sentence indicates that Maria's focus on her footwork started a month ago and is something she is still doing actively.

Match Preparations.

David has been studying his opponents' games this week. Here, David is currently engaged in Analyzing his competitors, emphasizing the ongoing nature of his preparation.

Recovery Practices.

Lily has been recovering from her injury since last season.

This highlights that her recovery is an ongoing process that started previously and is still relevant now.

Engaging with the Present Perfect Continuous.

As you practice on the court, actively engage with the present perfect continuous by describing your own experiences. Here are some prompts to encourage you:

Describe your training routine.

I have been focusing on my backhand for the last two weeks.

I have been taking extra lessons on strategy recently.

Talk about your fitness:

I have been running to improve my speed lately.

I have been doing strength training to boost my performance.

Reflect on your competitions:

I have been participating in tournaments every weekend this month.

I have been preparing for the championship match since last summer.

Exercises to Practice.

To reinforce your understanding of the present perfect continuous in a tennis context, try out the following exercises:

Fill in the Blanks:

Complete the sentences using the present perfect continuous form of the verbs provided.

My friend has been playing tennis every Sunday for the past year.

The coach (design) ____ new drills to help us improve.

Create Your Own Sentences.

Think of your current activities related to tennis and make sentences in the present perfect continuous.

Conversation Practice

Pair up with a partner and take turns asking each other about your tennis practices using the present perfect continuous structure. For example: What have you been working on during your last training sessions?
As you continue your journey of learning English through tennis, remember the power of the present perfect continuous. It allows you to articulate ongoing actions, providing clarity and context during discussions about your training and experiences on the court. The more you incorporate this tense into your practice, the more confident you will grow in your language skills. Now, grab your racket and start using the present perfect continuous to talk about your game—both on and off the court!

The Past Perfect Simple.

Tennis is more than just a sport; it represents a path of learning, strategy, and personal development. As we explore the English language through tennis, we come across various verb tenses that enable us to convey actions in a sequential manner. In this chapter, we will concentrate on the past perfect simple, an essential component of the English language that helps us talk about actions that were finished prior to specific moments in the past.

Understanding the Past Perfect Simple.

The past perfect simple is formed using the auxiliary verb "had" followed by the past participle of the main verb. This tense is particularly useful when you want to emphasize that one event happened before another event in the past. Here's a brief structure:

Subject + had + past participle

Example: "Before the match, Maria had practiced her serve."

In this example, "had practiced" indicates that Maria's practice occurred before the event of the match.

Contextualizing with Tennis

Let's illustrate the past perfect simple in various tennis scenarios, making it easier for you to understand and relate to.

Example 1: The Early Arrivals.

Imagine two players, John and Sarah, preparing for their big match. John arrived at the court early, while Sarah was still getting ready. You might say, "By the time Sarah arrived, John had already warmed up." This sentence showcases the past perfect simple as it clearly indicates that John's action of warming up took place before Sarah's arrival.

Example 2: Conditionals in Tennis Training.

Often, players reflect on their training sessions while analyzing their performance. Here's how we can use the past perfect simple in this context: "If I had practiced my backhand more, I would have won the tournament." In this statement, the use of "had practiced" illustrates how the training was completed before the anticipated outcome of winning the tournament.

Example 3: Learning from Mistakes.

Every athlete learns from their mistakes. Suppose you hear a player discuss their previous matches: "I had made several errors in the first set, which affected my performance." In this case, "had made" emphasizes that the errors occurred before their current reflection on the match.

More Examples in Action.

To gain a thorough understanding of the past perfect simple, let's explore a few more tennis-related sentences:

- "They had discussed their strategies before stepping onto the court."
- "After she had played in several tournaments, Julia felt more confident."
- "He realized that he had forgotten to bring his water bottle."

Each of these sentences demonstrates the past perfect simple effectively, showcasing the sequence of events that took place leading up to a specific moment.

Practice Makes Perfect.

To reinforce your learning, consider the following exercises focused on the past perfect simple in a tennis context:

Fill in the Blanks.

- When she arrived, her opponent (already / warm up).
- By the time the match started, the crowd (gather / outside).
- He showed up late because he (forget / his racket).

Create Your Own Sentences.

The past perfect simple is an essential tool in the English language, particularly for narrating events and experiences. By incorporating tennis scenarios into your learning, you can better grasp this tense while enhancing your vocabulary and understanding of English. Practice these structures, and soon enough, you'll be discussing tennis matches with fluency and confidence, both on and off the court!

Now, as you lace up your tennis shoes and head for the court, remember to leverage the power of past perfect simple in your conversations. Happy learning!

Past perfect continuous in a tennis setting.

Let's move on to the past perfect continuous. The past perfect continuous describes something that happened in the past, but describing an ongoing action. The past perfect continuous is used to talk about a temporary past event that happened before another event or action took place: for example: Venus had been walking to the court when she hurt her foot.

The Past Perfect Continuous.

Now we will explore the **past perfect continuous tense**—a grammatical structure that will enhance your ability to describe past events in English, especially in the context of tennis.

Understanding the Past Perfect Continuous.

The **past perfect continuous tense** is used to discuss actions that were ongoing up until a specific moment in the past. It highlights the duration of past actions before another action occurred. This tense can effectively convey the circumstances leading to an event, making your storytelling richer and more engaging.

Structure of the Past Perfect Continuous.

The structure of the past perfect continuous is:

had been + verb-ing.

- **Subject**: The person or thing performing the action.
- **had**: The auxiliary verb indicating the past perfect aspect.
- **been**: The past participle of "to be."
- **verb-ing**: The present participle form of the main verb.

Instances in a Tennis Setting.

Let's delve into some tennis-specific examples to illustrate the past perfect continuous tense.

1. **Venus had been practicing on the court when she heard the announcement about the tournament.**
   This sentence indicates that Venus's practice was ongoing before she heard the announcement, emphasizing the duration of her practice.
2. **The team had been training hard for weeks before they competed in the championship.**
   Here, the focus is on the extended period of training leading up to the championship. It provides context and shows dedication.
3. **I had been watching the match from the sidelines before it started to rain.**
   This example is useful for situations where the ongoing activity (watching) was occurring before another event (the rain) interrupted it.

Using the Past Perfect Continuous Effectively.

To effectively use the past perfect continuous tense in your tennis conversations or writing, consider the following tips:

- **Context is Key**: Ensure that your sentences convey the timeline of events clearly. Using transition words like "before," "when," or "by the time" can help clarify the sequence.
- **Describing Emotions and Experiences**: Use this tense to express feelings or states resulting from prolonged actions. For instance, "I had been feeling anxious before the big match," emphasizes the build-up of emotions over time.
- **Adding Depth to Narratives**: When telling a story about a match, practice, or tennis lesson, incorporating the past perfect continuous can add depth to your descriptions. For example, "We had been discussing strategy for hours before the match began."

'Training Activities'

To help solidify your understanding of the past perfect continuous, try these practice exercises:

1. Create three sentences about a famous tennis player using the
2. past perfect continuous.
3. Write a short paragraph describing a day of training at the tennis academy, incorporating at least two examples of the past perfect continuous tense.
4. Share your favorite tennis memory using the past perfect continuous. Focus on what you were doing prior to a significant event in that memory.

The past perfect continuous tense is an invaluable tool for any English learner, especially in the context of tennis. It allows you to articulate ongoing actions and circumstances leading to events in a nuanced way. By practicing this tense, you can improve your storytelling skills and engage with others more effectively.

As you continue your journey from court to classroom, keep integrating these grammatical structures in your conversations and written exercises. Happy learning, and may your linguistic skills flourish alongside your love for tennis!

Future Tenses.

Introduction to Future Tenses.

In English, we use different tenses to express when actions occur. Among them, the future tense allow us to discuss events that have not yet happened. This chapter will focus on the Future Simple tense, particularly in a tennis context, helping you to learn English while enjoying the sport.

What is Future Simple?

The Future Simple tense is used to describe actions that will take place in the future. It is formed using the modal verb "will" followed by the base form of the verb. For example:

- **Structure**: Subject + will + base verb
- **Example**: He will serve the ball.

This tense is straightforward and often used in everyday conversations. In tennis, we can use this structure to talk about future match plans, predictions, or intentions.

Examples of Future Simple in a Tennis Setting.

Predictions

- "Maria will win the match."
- "They will play very well in the tournament."

Plans

- "I will practice my backhand tomorrow."
- "We will meet at the court at 10 AM."

Intentions.

- "I will participate in the local tennis championship."
- "He will join a training session next week."

Practice Makes Perfect.

To master the Future Simple tense, it's important to practice. Here are some exercises that can help you reinforce what you've learned

Exercise 1: Fill in the Blanks.

Complete the sentences using the Future Simple tense:

1. Tomorrow, I __ (to play) tennis at the club.
2. My friend __ (to join) me for a doubles match.
3. They __ (to train) for the regional championships next month.
4. We __ (to watch) the final match on Sunday.

Exercise 2: Create Your Own Sentences.

Think about your upcoming tennis plans and write four sentences in the Future Simple tense:

1. I will __.
2. My coach will __.
3. We will __.
4. I believe I will __.

Dialogue Practice.

Practicing dialogue can also help in learning tenses. Here's a short conversation between two tennis players discussing their future:

Player 1: What will you do this weekend?

Player 2: I will train at the new facility. How about you?

Player 1: I will have a friendly match with my neighbor.

Player 2: Sounds great! I hope we will meet in the finals of the tournament next month.

Mastering the Future Simple tense is an essential step in learning English, particularly when discussing sports like tennis. By using the structure outlined in this chapter and practicing with the provided exercises, you'll be able to confidently talk about your tennis future in English. Whether discussing your upcoming matches, training sessions, or predictions, the Future Simple tense is a powerful tool in your linguistic arsenal. Keep practicing, and you'll see improvement in no time!

Future Continuous.

Learning English through the context of tennis can be both engaging and effective. Now, we will explore the future continuous tense.

What is Future Continuous?

The future continuous tense is used to describe actions that will be in progress at a specific time in the future. It emphasizes the duration of the action rather than its completion. The structure of the future continuous is as follows:

Subject + will be + verb-ing (present participle)

Examples.

"Sofia will be walking to the court at 4 PM."

"They will be practicing their serves during the lesson."

"The coach will be analysing their performances after the match."

Using Future Continuous in a Tennis Context

Now, let's put this into practice with some engaging tennis scenarios:

1. Pre-Match Preparation.

Imagine a typical match day at the local tennis club. The players are busy preparing for their upcoming matches, and their actions can be described using the future continuous tense.

"At 1 PM, the players will be warming up on the court."

"Sofia will be stretching her muscles to prevent injury."

"The umpire will be checking the match schedule for any changes."

2. During the Match.

As the match unfolds, players remain focused on their game, and we can use future continuous to describe what they will be doing.

"In the second set, Sofia will be serving to her opponent."

"The spectators will be cheering when a great point is played."

"During the break, the coach will be discussing strategies with the players."

3. Post-Match Analysis.

After the match, analysis and reflection are crucial for improvement. The future continuous can portray the players' activities during this time.

"Tomorrow, Sofia will be reviewing her performance with her coach."

"The team will be watching video footage of the match to identify weaknesses."

"By this time next week, they will be training harder based on the feedback."

Common Mistakes with Future Continuous.

As with any grammatical structure, learners often make errors when using the future continuous. Here are some common mistakes to watch out for:

1. Incorrect Time Specifiers.

Be cautious of using time expressions that do not align with the action being described. Remember that future continuous should refer to an action happening at a specific time in the future.

Incorrect: "They will be finished their game by 6 PM."

Correct: "They will be finishing their game by 6 PM."

2. Negation Errors.

When negating the future continuous, make sure to place "not" correctly in the structure.

Incorrect: "Sofia will not being serving during the match."

Correct: "Sofia will not be serving during the match."

Practice Exercises.

To reinforce your understanding of the future continuous tense, here are some practice exercises set in a tennis context:

Exercise 1: Fill in the Blanks

Complete the sentences using the future continuous tense.

At 5 PM, the players __ (practice) their serves.

During the tournament, the spectators __ (watch) the matches in excitement.

Next week, Sofia __ (train) with a new coach.

Exercise 2: Create Your Sentences.

Now, think of your own sentences using the future continuous tense in a tennis context. Be sure to include specific times for your actions.

The future continuous tense is a vital aspect of English grammar, especially for language learners enthusiastic about tennis. By understanding how to frame this tense within a sports context, you not only improve your language skills but also make the learning process more enjoyable. Remember to practice by visualizing tennis-related scenarios in your mind, allowing a seamless blend of language and sport. Happy learning!

Future Perfect Simple.

Understanding the Future Perfect Simple

The Future Perfect Simple is a grammatical tense used to discuss actions that will be completed at or before a specified point in the future. It is formed using "will have" plus the past participle of the verb. This tense is particularly useful when you want to communicate expectations or predictions about future achievements.

Structure

Formula: Subject + will have + past participle + (additional information)

For example.

"She will have improved her serve by next season."

We are going to explore the Future Perfect Simple through the lens of tennis, making it relatable and engaging for English learners.

Contextualizing the Future Perfect Simple in Tennis.

To better grasp this tense, let's visualize various scenarios within the sport of tennis. Consider the following sentences that illustrate the application of the Future Perfect Simple:

Training Continuous Improvement.

"By the end of the month, you will have practiced your backhand 20 times."

Explanation: This suggests that the action of practicing will occur multiple times and will be completed by the end of the month.

Tournament Preparation.

"By the time the tournament starts, he will have developed a new strategy for the final match."

Explanation: This indicates that the player will have completed the development of a strategy before the tournament begins.

Setting Goals.

"By the end of the season, she will have won three tournaments."

Explanation: It emphasizes the completion of the action (winning tournaments) by the season's end.

Using the Future Perfect Simple with Time Markers.

In tennis, time markers are essential for setting deadlines and goals. Using phrases like "by tomorrow," "by the end of the week," or "by next year" can guide the use of the Future Perfect Simple. Here are some more examples:

"By 3 PM tomorrow, he will have finished his physical conditioning session."

"By 2025, the club will have equipped all its courts with new nets."

Each of these examples specifies a future time frame, which helps learners visualize when the actions will be completed.

Exercises to Practice the Future Perfect Simple

To reinforce learning, here are some exercises. Encourage students to create their examples using the Future Perfect Simple in tennis contexts.

Fill in the Blanks.

By next week, I __ (to play) at least five practice matches.

By the end of the year, she __ (to qualify) for the national finals.

They __ (to improve) their doubles team dynamics before the championship.

Create Sentences.

Ask students to formulate sentences using the Future Perfect Simple. They might consider scenarios like:

Their journey to a championship.

Training sessions leading to significant matches.

Achieving personal bests in their game.

For example:

"By the end of the summer, I will have mastered my serve."

The Future Perfect Simple is a powerful tense that conveys the completion of actions within time constraints. By associating this tense with tennis, learners can better grasp its application, enriching their vocabulary and enhancing their grammatical understanding. Whether discussing training regimens, goals, or tournament outcomes, the Future Perfect Simple allows for effective communication of future achievements. As we move forward, remember to apply this exciting tense in your tennis-related conversations and writings.

Future Perfect Continuous.

Understanding the Future Perfect Continuous Tense.

The future perfect continuous tense is a valuable tool in English that allows us to express an action that will have been ongoing for a certain duration at a specific point in the future. This grammatical structure is essential for conveying the concept of time and duration, as it combines aspects of both the future perfect and the present continuous tenses.

Structure of the Future Perfect Continuous.

To form the future perfect continuous tense, we follow this structure:

Subject + will have been + verb (base form + -ing) + duration (time expression)

For instance, let's consider the following formulation:

Jasmine will have been walking to the court for 15 minutes when she arrives.

In this sentence:

Subject: Jasmine

Auxiliary Verbs: will have been

Main Verb: walking

Duration: for 15 minutes

This tells us that by the time Jasmine arrives at the court, she will have already spent 15 minutes walking there.

Key Examples in Tennis Context.

Let's explore some tennis-related examples that illustrate the use of the future perfect continuous tense. These examples will not only provide context for understanding the tense but will also engage tennis enthusiasts in learning English!

By the end of this season, Maria will have been training with her coach for five years.

This sentence emphasizes Maria's long-term commitment to her training, indicating a continuous effort leading up to the end of the current season.

Next month, John will have been participating in tournaments for two years straight.

Here, we highlight John's dedication to competing in tennis tournaments continuously over a significant period.

By the time the major match starts, the players will have been warming up for at least 30 minutes.

This example illustrates the preparation that players undertake before a match, ensuring they are physically ready.

In 2025, the tennis academy will have been offering programs for young athletes for a decade.

This sentence reflects on the academy's longevity in providing educational resources and training opportunities for aspiring players.

Tips for Using the Future Perfect Continuous.

When using the future perfect continuous tense, consider the following tips:

Be Specific with Time Expressions: It often helps to specify the duration or time frame to make the sentence clear. Words like "for," "since," and "by" are essential for giving the right context.

Practice with Real-Life Scenarios: Using tennis as a backdrop, you can create various scenarios to express what players will have been experiencing or doing at given points in the future.

Combine with Other Tenses: Experiment by combining the future perfect continuous with other tenses to see how interconnections can enhance your English skills and storytelling.

Practice Activities.

Activity 1: Fill in the Blanks

Complete the following sentences using the future perfect continuous tense.

By the end of the tournament, Sam __ (practice) for over 20 hours.

By next summer, I __ (play) tennis for three years.

When she competes in the finals, Ana __ (train) every day for a month.

Activity 2: Create Your Own Sentences

Think of a tennis player of your choice and write three sentences in the future perfect continuous tense about their training, competitions, or experiences leading up to a significant event.

____.

____.

____.

By utilizing the future perfect continuous tense, learners can refine their English skills while embracing the dynamic world of tennis. Whether discussing a player's training regime or reflecting on their career, this tense provides an essential framework for expressing ongoing actions in relation to future events. With practice and engagement, mastering this tense will enhance your proficiency in English, making your communication—on and off the tennis court—more fluid and expressive.

Conditionals.

In English, conditionals are crucial for expressing possibilities and hypothetical situations. In this chapter, we will delve into the four types of conditionals—zero, first, second, and third—and explore how they can be used in a tennis context. By linking these grammatical structures to familiar tennis scenarios, you will not only improve your language skills but also deepen your understanding of the sport.

Zero Conditional.

The zero conditional is used for general truths or facts. It is structured with the present simple tense in both the "if" clause and the main clause.

Structure.

If + present simple, present simple.

Example in Tennis.

If you hit a forehand correctly, the ball goes over the net.

If it rains, the match will be postponed.

In both examples, the statements are universally true. The zero conditional is perfect for expressing rules or facts about tennis.

First Conditional.

The first conditional is used for real and possible situations in the future. It combines the present simple in the "if" clause with the future simple in the main clause.

Structure.

If + present simple, will + base form of the verb.

Example in Tennis.

If I practice my serve, I will improve my game.

If she wins this match, she will qualify for the finals.

These sentences show real scenarios that could happen depending on current actions or situations. The first conditional is fantastic for discussing future outcomes based on present actions.

Second Conditional.

The second conditional is for hypothetical situations that are unlikely to happen. It uses the past simple in the "if" clause and "would" with the base form of the verb in the main clause.

Structure.

If + past simple, would + base form of the verb.

Example in Tennis.

> If I had a coach, I would win more tournaments.
>
> If he played tennis every day, he would become a pro.

These scenarios are hypothetical; they express what could happen if circumstances were different. The second conditional is essential for discussing dreams and aspirations related to tennis

Third Conditional.

The third conditional is used to talk about situations in the past that did not happen. It employs the past perfect in the "if" clause and "would have" with the past participle in the main clause.

Structure.

> If I had trained harder, I would have won that match.
>
> If she had practiced her backhand, she would have taken the title.

Here, we reflect on past actions and their missed opportunities, focusing on what could have been in the realm of tennis.

Mixed Conditionals.

Mixed conditionals combine elements from different types of conditionals to express complex thoughts.

Example.

If I had won the competition (past), I would be playing in the finals now (present).

This structure allows for a rich discussion about different time frames and possibilities. It is particularly useful when considering the impact of past events on current situations, especially in sports.

Understanding and using conditionals correctly is vital for effective communication in English, particularly in specific contexts like tennis. By associating conditionals with relatable tennis scenarios, you can improve both your English language skills and your appreciation for the sport. Practice each type of conditional with your own tennis-related examples to further enhance your learning experience. With consistent use and practice, you will be able to articulate your thoughts and hypotheses about the game and your own journey in tennis fluently. Keep hitting those serves and those sentences and this is the end of the Grammar Chapter, well done!

Section Three.
Tennis Training for Performance.

Performance athletes demonstrate both dedication and skill in their sport. It's important to understand the distinction between potential and talent; while players may possess talent, they might not have the commitment and determination needed to realize their full potential. In tennis, a player must combine physical ability, mental resilience, emotional strength, technical proficiency, competitive skills, a passion for the game, and an ambition to achieve the highest level. This section of the book aims to be a cornerstone for understanding how to approach your training and behavior in a performance environment, along with the framework to achieve it: let's start with the warm-up—agility, balance, coordination, speed, and strength (ABCSS)

In the fast-paced realm of tennis, where each racket swing can determine success or failure, the transition from the court to the classroom is filled with valuable lessons. Training goes beyond mere drills; it represents a commitment to nurturing an athlete's physical, mental, and emotional well-being. This section examines the core of training within a performance context, revealing the delicate balance between talent and potential, and demonstrating how systematic approaches can significantly enhance your game. Before we dive into specific training methods, it's essential to grasp the critical ideas of commitment and talent.

For performance athletes, talent signifies the natural abilities that allow for skilled play; however, it is commitment—the unwavering drive and determination—that converts innate talent into outstanding performance. Imagine two athletes with comparable skills: one may have remarkable reflexes and a natural swing, while the other shows steadfast dedication and an unquenchable thirst for improvement. Typically, the latter, through hard work and perseverance, will outshine the former in reaching their objectives. This distinction is vital; potential remains unrealized without the effort and dedication needed to bring it to fruition.

The Fundamentals of a Tennis Player.

To succeed in the competitive world of tennis, players need to develop a combination of physical, mental, emotional, and technical skills. Let's take a closer look at these components: Tennis is not merely a sport; it represents a lifestyle that fosters not only an athlete's physical capabilities but also their emotional and mental strength. When aspiring tennis players step onto the court, they confront not only the challenge of competing against others but also embark on a personal journey of self-discovery. This discussion highlights the crucial attributes that a tennis player must develop to excel both on the court and in life.

At the core of every accomplished tennis player is a steadfast dedication to physical fitness. The sport requires a distinct blend of speed, agility, endurance, and strength. Each player must condition their body to react instinctively, quickly adjusting to the game's pace. Consistent and diverse training sessions, including footwork drills and strength training, enable players to build the muscular endurance needed for demanding matches. Additionally, flexibility is vital; it helps prevent injuries and allows for greater movement, crucial for reaching challenging shots. Nonetheless, physical training alone is not enough. Nutrition is essential for an athlete's performance. A diet rich in vital nutrients provides energy, aids recovery, and promotes overall health. Tennis players must pay attention to their hydration to ensure optimal performance. By treating their bodies as finely tuned machines, players can enhance their effectiveness both on and off the court. This awareness prepares them for the demands of competition and instills valuable life lessons about discipline and self-care, encouraging a well-rounded approach to their athletic journey.

Mental strength is a crucial trait of successful tennis players. As the game progresses and pressure intensifies, players must remain focused and composed. The stress of close matches can lead to anxiety and self-doubt, making mental training strategies essential. Techniques such as visualization, positive self-talk, and mindfulness can help players stay grounded and calm, even in high-pressure situations. Resilience is a vital aspect of a tennis player's mental makeup. The ability to recover from setbacks, whether it's a lost match or an injury, defines the character of a true champion. Learning to view failure as a stepping stone rather than an obstacle is crucial. Through this perspective, players enhance not only their skills on the court but also their ability to face life's challenges with dignity and determination. This path of resilience transforms tennis players into leaders—individuals capable of overcoming adversity and inspiring others, both in tennis and beyond.

Beyond the physical and mental aspects lies emotional intelligence—an often-overlooked attribute in the world of sports. Tennis players encounter a whirlwind of emotions during a match, from elation to frustration and everything in between. Understanding and mastering these emotions is crucial for success. While tennis is predominantly an individual sport, players can also develop a sense of empathy and camaraderie. Learning from fellow players, celebrating their successes, and supporting them during tough times cultivates resilience within the community.

By embracing emotional intelligence, players enhance their social skills and adaptability, critical components in today's interconnected world. As athletes navigate the highs and lows of competition, they grow emotionally, establishing connections that transcend the court. In synthesizing these elements—physical training, mental fortitude, and emotional intelligence—tennis players emerge as multifaceted individuals. The journey from court to classroom is not merely about mastering the mechanics of the game; it is an immersive experience that shapes the character and resilience of each athlete. In this harmonious blend of skills, players learn invaluable lessons about dedication, teamwork, and perseverance. Whether competing at the highest levels or teaching the next generation, tennis players carry these lessons into all facets of life, embodying the essence of a true athlete. This is not just a story about tennis; it's about transformation, illustrating how the court serves as a classroom for life.

Physical Capability.

Tennis is a highly demanding physical sport. Players require agility to move quickly around the court, strength for powerful serves, and endurance to sustain their performance during long matches. Focusing on fitness through specific conditioning routines is essential to enable players to perform at their peak. Often referred to as the sport of a thousand matches, tennis goes beyond just skillful strokes and strategic play. Fundamentally, it presents an exciting physical challenge that tests and enhances a player's physical capabilities.

As athletes pursue errant balls around the court, they exhibit a combination of agility, strength, and endurance—each vital to their overall performance. This chapter will delve into the significance of physical conditioning in tennis and offer specific routines that players can implement to ensure optimal performance on the court. Agility is defined as a player's ability to change direction quickly while keeping balance and control. It enables a player to smoothly navigate the baseline, jump for a volley, and react effortlessly to an opponent's unpredictability. In tennis, where every moment is crucial, agility drills can be the deciding factor between reaching a ball or letting it pass by.

Essential Agility Exercises.

Position two cones approximately 10 feet apart. Begin at one cone and shuffle laterally to the opposite cone, then return. Focus on maintaining speed and control. Include this drill in your routine for around 15 minutes, emphasizing rapid foot movement and stability.

Tennis Ladder Drills: Utilize an agility ladder to execute different footwork patterns such as in-and-out hops or side steps. This exercise enhances your foot speed and promotes rapid transitions that are crucial in tennis.

Arrange cones in a T-shape. Run to the center cone, then sidestep to the side cones and return to the center. This exercise simulates the quick directional movements needed in a match.

Strength: Powering Your Game.

Strength is crucial for serving, delivering powerful groundstrokes, and performing effective volleys. A well-conditioned player can produce greater power and also reduce the risk of injury by strengthening muscles and joints.

Fundamental Strength Workouts.

Bench Press: This traditional exercise enhances upper body strength, essential for an effective serve. Target three sets of eight repetitions, gradually increasing the weight as your strength progresses.

Squats: Strengthening your lower body is essential for increasing power in your shots and ensuring a stable foundation. Complete three sets of ten repetitions with correct form to improve leg strength.

Planks: Core strength is essential for your overall stability and balance. Incorporate core exercises such as front and side planks to build a strong foundation, holding each position for 30 seconds to one minute.

Endurance: Lasting Through the Match.

Regardless of a player's agility or strength, the lack of endurance can lead to rapid fatigue. In extended matches, a player's capacity to stay focused and sustain peak performance relies heavily on their cardiovascular fitness.

Tips for Endurance Training

Interval Training: Add sprint intervals to your cardio workout. By alternating 30 seconds of high-intensity sprints with one minute of slow jogging, you improve cardiovascular fitness and replicate the stop-and-go dynamics of tennis.

Long-Distance Running: Dedicate one session a week to running for extended periods (30-60 minutes) at a moderate pace. This builds endurance, ensuring you can maintain your energy levels throughout the match.

Circuit Training: Combine strength and endurance in a circuit that includes exercises like push-ups, burpees, and jumping jacks. Aim to perform each exercise for 30 seconds, resting briefly between sets. This not only builds muscle but also boosts aerobic fitness. Physical fitness in tennis is not merely an enhancement; it is a necessity. A player's success on the court is intrinsically linked to their physical conditioning. By incorporating specific agility drills, strength exercises, and endurance training into your routine, you set the stage for exceptional performance. Remember, the most skilled player on the court is not just the one with the best technique, but the one who is physically prepared to execute their strategy with finesse. Embrace the physical side of tennis, and you'll find that your game will reach exhilarating new heights

Mental Toughness.

In tennis, the court transcends a mere physical battleground; it serves as a psychological arena where the mind relentlessly strives to outshine opponents. The pressure faced by players—whether it's match points, the burden of expectations, or the unpredictability of rivals—requires a strong mental game that parallels the physical skills honed through extensive training. This chapter will delve into how mental toughness can be developed through visualization and focus techniques, enabling athletes to keep their composure, respond constructively to challenges, and perform under duress.

Tennis stands out for its individualistic nature; unlike team sports, a player faces an opponent alone. This solitude can be both freeing and intimidating. Each match unfolds a narrative where the result hinges not solely on skill but also on mental resilience. Mental toughness acts as the armor players don in this intellectual duel on the court. Those who can overcome their doubts and fears can rise above adversity, turning challenges into chances for personal growth. Players encounter various pressures during a match, including the crowd's noise, expectations from coaches and fans, and the internal dialogue that can either inspire or hinder performance. The ability to maneuver through these mental obstacles often separates good players from exceptional ones. This is where mental conditioning becomes crucial.

Techniques for Visualization.

Visualization is a potent technique that athletes have utilized for years to improve their performance. It entails mentally practicing particular situations to ready both the mind and body for actual execution. For tennis players, this might involve imagining themselves successfully serving an ace or flawlessly hitting a backhand down the line.

Forming a Clear Mental Picture.

To make the most of visualization, players need to:

Locate a tranquil area. Seek out a cozy place, free from interruptions, where you can unwind.

Shut your eyes. This aids in eliminating external distractions, enabling you to concentrate on your inner thoughts.

Envision intricate scenarios. Visualize the court, the sensation of the racket in your grip, and the cheers of the audience. Involve all your senses to create vibrant and immersive mental images.

Make it a habit to practice consistently. Just like physical training, visualization needs regular practice to be truly effective. Integrate it into your daily routine, so that mental rehearsal becomes instinctive.

Visualizing successful outcomes helps players alleviate anxiety, boost their confidence, and get ready to make decisive moves under pressure on the court.

Focus Training.

Mental focus is an essential aspect of mental toughness. In the intense world of competitive tennis, staying concentrated can be just as difficult as perfecting a difficult shot. Focus training is about enhancing the capacity to direct and maintain attention on the current task while reducing distractions.

Methods for Enhancing Concentration.

Mindfulness Meditation. Engaging in mindfulness can improve your concentration. It helps individuals remain in the moment, grounding their attention in the present instead of dwelling on past errors or anticipating future results.

Breathing Techniques. Practicing controlled breathing can soothe anxiety and enhance focus. Taking deep, steady breaths before key moments can help players centre themselves and sharpen their concentration.

Establish Clear Objectives. In your practice sessions, focus on short-term goals related to your performance instead of the score. For example, strive to get 80% of your serves into the service box, helping you to focus on the technical aspects of your execution rather than the outcome.

Encouraging Self-Talk. Fostering a conversation of support instead of criticism can help maintain a strong mindset for a player. Swap negative thoughts for positive affirmations that boost confidence and resilience.

The combination of physical skill and mental strength is crucial for achieving success in tennis. By adopting visualization methods and concentration exercises, players can build the mental fortitude needed to excel under pressure. The insights gained on the court apply to more than just tennis; they echo in educational settings and throughout life, highlighting that with the proper mindset, we can overcome any obstacle. By fostering mental toughness, we enhance our abilities as athletes while also becoming more resilient individuals, ready to tackle life's challenges.

The mental aspect of tennis is just as crucial as the physical side. Players face numerous pressures, including the stress of match points, the burden of expectations, and the unpredictability of their opponents. By cultivating mental resilience with visualization strategies and concentration exercises, players can stay composed, respond effectively to challenges, and excel under pressure.

Emotional Resilience.

Tennis is a game filled with intense emotions. Players can soar with victory and plunge into disappointment in just moments. Building emotional resilience—understanding and managing emotions—enables athletes to stay centered, recover from setbacks, and keep their sights on performance goals. It's not merely a test of physical skill; it's a mental challenge. The emotional dynamics of a match can change rapidly—an incredible ace might be followed by an uncharacteristic double fault, and the excitement of winning a point can swiftly turn into frustration over a missed chance. This emotional fluctuation can be particularly overwhelming for young athletes who are still learning to balance their sporting ambitions with personal development.

Cultivating emotional resilience is essential not only for achieving success on the court but also for fostering resilience in everyday life. In tennis, emotions can run high. Players often feel exhilarated after executing a perfect shot or distressed by mistakes that seem unexpected. These emotional peaks and valleys can lead to two significant results: improved performance or crippling self-doubt. The ability to navigate this emotional journey effectively distinguishes the good players from the great ones. Mastering the management of emotions is a skill that can be developed, enabling players to channel their intense feelings into greater focus and enhanced performance.

The Significance of Managing Emotions.

Recognizing that emotions are a natural part of performance is the initial step to developing emotional resilience in tennis. Rather than trying to suppress or overlook feelings, players should embrace them. Mindfulness practices can facilitate this acceptance, allowing players to observe their emotional states without judgment. By identifying emotions like excitement, anger, or fear as they surface, players can improve their ability to manage their responses.

Methods for Developing Emotional Resilience.

Mindfulness Practice.

Engaging in mindfulness practices like meditation and focused breathing can assist players in remaining present. These techniques enable them to notice their thoughts and emotions without becoming overwhelmed, fostering a sense of tranquility and concentration during high-pressure games.

Encouraging Self-Dialogue.

The stories we create in our minds can greatly influence our emotional reactions. It's important for players to develop a routine of positive self-talk, transforming negative thoughts into supportive affirmations. Expressions such as "I am capable" or "This situation does not determine my worth" can enhance confidence and help avoid the downward spiral that comes with failure.

Imagery.

Visualization serves as a strong technique that allows athletes to envision themselves successfully performing skills and managing emotional hurdles. This mental practice equips them for actual scenarios, boosting their confidence and emotional readiness for competition.

Regularity and Dependability.

Establishing a consistent on-court routine can offer players a sense of structure and reassurance. Whether it involves a particular serving technique or a pre-match warm-up, a regular approach aids players in coping with anxiety and staying focused, which directly contributes to their emotional stability.

Developing emotional strength doesn't have to be done alone. Coaches, teammates, and family members can significantly contribute to a player's resilience. Engaging in open discussions about emotions, exchanging experiences, and seeking guidance from seasoned players can promote personal development. Highlighting the value of a supportive atmosphere—where players can freely share their fears, successes, and setbacks—can lead to meaningful growth.

The abilities gained from striving for emotional strength in tennis reach well beyond the sport itself. The lessons in emotional management, resilience, and self-awareness are crucial in educational environments and in life overall. As students navigate the challenges of competition, they also develop skills that benefit them in their studies, relationships, and future professional endeavors.

Emotional resilience is a crucial element for achieving success in both athletics and personal life, particularly in a demanding sport like tennis. By accepting emotional fluctuations, practicing mindfulness, maintaining positive self-dialogue, using visualization techniques, and building solid support networks, athletes can develop the ability to excel under pressure. The transition from the court to the classroom—equipped with the tools of emotional control—paves the way for not just improved tennis skills, but also for becoming more resilient individuals prepared to face life's obstacles.

Technical Skills.

Every exceptional tennis player is built on a strong foundation of technical skills. Mastering serves, volleys, and groundstrokes must go hand in hand with strategic gameplay and a clear awareness of personal strengths and weaknesses. Consistent practice, constructive feedback, and ongoing refinement of these skills create the toolkit needed for a capable player. Tennis combines skill, strategy, and finesse. Whether you are a novice eager to grasp the fundamentals or an experienced player looking to enhance your techniques, a solid understanding of essential technical skills is vital for success on the court. Additionally, incorporating these skills into a well-structured learning environment can greatly improve your overall game. This chapter delves into the core technical skills in tennis, examines their practical application on the court, and explores how they can be effectively taught in a classroom setting.

Grip and Stance.

The Significance of Grip.

The grip is perhaps the most essential element of playing tennis. It establishes the basis for every shot, whether delivering a strong serve or executing a delicate volley. Various grips exist, including the Continental, Eastern, Western, and Semi-Western, each designed for specific shot types.

Continental Grip: Ideal for serves and volleys, offering flexibility.

Eastern Grip: Frequently utilized for forehands, allowing for both topspin and flat shots.

Western Grip: Perfect for producing significant topspin, particularly on forehands.

Encouraging players to try out various grips can assist them in finding what is the most comfortable and effective for their individual playing style.

Position and Stability.

A correct stance provides stability and preparedness for any shot. There are mainly two types of stances: open and closed. An open stance enables players to face the net directly, facilitating faster lateral movement. In contrast, a closed stance has the body turned sideways, which can be more advantageous for executing strong groundstrokes.

Classroom Tip: Use diagrams to illustrate the different stances. Practicing in front of a mirror can help students evaluate their posture and make necessary adjustments.

Movement techniques.

Speed Across the Court

Effective footwork is essential in tennis. It requires moving efficiently to get into the best position for the next shot. Important footwork patterns include:

Lateral Movements: Helpful for side steps.

Crossover Steps: Crucial for quickly approaching or distancing yourself from the net.

Split Step: A preparatory action that enables players to spring into action as the opponent hits the ball.

Agility Drills.

Including agility drills in practice improves footwork abilities. Basic exercises such as ladder drills, cone sprints, and shadowing can enhance speed and coordination on the court.

Classroom Tip: Develop a timetable for agility exercises. Motivate students to establish personal objectives to monitor their progress over time.

Stroke Mechanics.

Forehand and Backhand

The forehand and backhand strokes constitute the core of the game.

Forehand.

The forehand is commonly seen as the most instinctive stroke. Essential elements consist of:

Preparation: Correctly placing the non-dominant hand above and angling the racket appropriately.

Swing Path: A fluid and steady swing that extends towards the target.

Backhand.

The backhand can be performed with either one hand or two and requires practice to perfect.

One-handed backhand: Provides extension and adaptability but demands precise timing and coordination.

A two-handed backhand provides stability and control, which makes it a favored option for beginners.

Classroom Tip: Utilizing video analysis can be a powerful educational resource. By having students observe their strokes, they can pinpoint areas where they need to improve.

Serve and Volley.

Perfecting the Serve

The serve plays a vital role in the game, frequently influencing the rhythm of play. Effective serving techniques include:

Trophy Position: Raising the racket to create leverage.

Ball Toss: The toss should be consistent and at the right height for optimal striking.

Volleys

Volleys are executed close to the net and require quick reflexes and foot positioning. Key aspects include:

Short backswing: For quick reactions.

Body positioning: Keeping the body behind the ball to direct it accurately.

Classroom Tip: Practice serving scenarios through role-play. Encourage students to discuss strategies for serving in high-pressure situations.

Technical skills in tennis extend beyond mere physical ability; they include mental strategies, preparation, and adaptability. Comprehending the details of grips, stances, footwork, stroke mechanics, and serving enables players to move from being casual fans to accomplished competitors. Incorporating these skills into a classroom environment can enhance the understanding of the game. Utilizing diverse teaching methods allows students to effectively apply their technical knowledge to achieve success on the court. The saying "practice makes perfect" holds true in both tennis and education.

A Passion for the Sport.

The most essential aspect is undoubtedly the love for the game. This passion drives perseverance, motivating players to overcome challenges and invest time in honing their skills. Such dedication, alongside other factors, is crucial. In the realm of sports, especially tennis, the key to every successful player often lies in one crucial element: a deep love for the game. This affection is not just a temporary feeling; it is a profound passion that goes beyond the court, influencing every part of a player's life. It fuels their ambitions, sparks their competitive spirit, and nurtures an unwavering desire to improve.

The Significance of Passion.

Passion is the ultimate motivator. For a tennis player, it serves as the fire that keeps burning, even when the challenges seem insurmountable. When faced with a long series of losses, a player driven by passion will not be dissuaded. Instead, they will view each setback as an opportunity to learn and grow. This resilient mindset is paramount to achieving excellence. The story of countless champions, from Serena Williams to Roger Federer, is one where love for the game led them to surmount obstacles and emerge stronger.

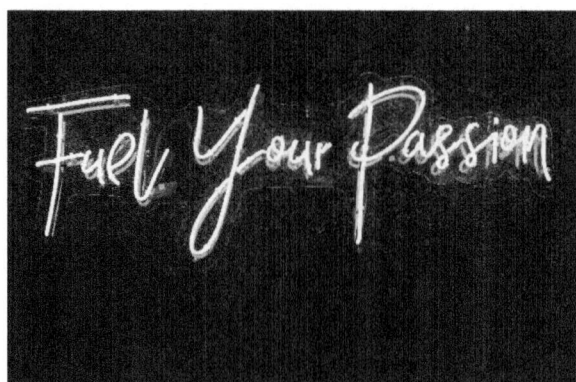

165 - 225

Conquering Challenges.

In an athlete's journey, facing challenges is a constant reality. Injuries, fierce rivals, and the immense pressure of competition can feel daunting. Yet, it is often a player's passion for tennis that draws them back to the court repeatedly. Consider a young athlete confronted with a potentially career-ending injury. While some might consider quitting, the dedicated player will put in the hard work needed for rehabilitation, motivated by the desire to once again hold the racket and experience the excitement of a great match. This commitment ultimately evolves into what psychologist's call "grit," a blend of passion and perseverance that is crucial for sustained success.

Commitment to Progress.

For tennis enthusiasts, every day offers a chance to improve. The court serves as a refuge where players can momentarily leave behind life's pressures, spending hours honing their serve, enhancing their footwork, or fine-tuning their tactics. Their passion for tennis drives them to create strict training schedules, frequently starting early and ending late. This unwavering commitment to progress highlights the bond between passion and dedication.

Consistent practice brings expertise.

The familiar saying "practice makes perfect" is particularly relevant in tennis. True enthusiasts of the game recognize that achieving mastery takes time. It involves honing skills, mastering techniques, and enhancing physical stamina, all of which demand extensive practice. The top players welcome this process. They find joy in the repetitive aspects of practice—not viewing it as a burden but as a vital part of their lives. Through this unwavering dedication, they grow not just as athletes, but also as people.

The Impact of Enthusiasm.

A player's passion for the game goes beyond their own success; it affects those nearby, motivating teammates and future players. A devoted player frequently emerges as a leader in their community, passing on their insights and excitement to younger athletes. This guidance can nurture a new wave of talent, who, inspired by those who came before them, find their own passion for the game.

Building a Legacy.

When a player infuses their journey with passion, they build a legacy that motivates others. Their tales of challenges, triumphs, and unwavering determination echo, fostering a belief in aspiring athletes that they too can reach greatness. Furthermore, the passion for the game crosses geographical limits, forging a universal link between players and fans. An unspoken connection develops among those committed to tennis—an awareness that the sport fundamentally represents much more than just winning.

The core of every exceptional tennis player is their passion for the sport. This enthusiasm is what inspires perseverance, motivates players to confront and conquer challenges, and propels them to enhance their abilities continually. Ultimately, it is this commitment to tennis that elevates aspiring athletes to the status of champions, enabling them to build legacies that inspire future generations. A genuine love for the game is not merely the starting point of a player's journey; it is the fundamental force that carries them through every triumph and setback, molding them into well-rounded athletes poised for greatness.

Organizing Your Training: The ABCSS Method.

Let's return to the basics to warm up (ABCSS), which is the first training element you should start with when you step onto the court before moving on to the second part of your session focused on game development.

Armed with the necessary attributes, players must then embrace a structured training regimen. Introducing the ABCSS system—Agility, Balance, Coordination, Speed, and Strength—serves as a holistic approach to preparation.

Agility: Improve your responsiveness and fluid movement on the court by incorporating ladder drills, cone exercises, and short sprints.

Balance: To enhance stability and control, which are essential for executing powerful strokes, incorporate balance boards or stability exercises into your routine.

Coordination: Incorporate hand-eye coordination exercises, such as using reaction balls or engaging in target practice, to enhance accuracy and precision in shooting.

Speed: Incorporate interval sprints and shadow drills to enhance explosive speed on the court, enabling players to reach the ball more quickly.

Strength: Develop strength training programs that concentrate on the essential muscle groups used in tennis, enabling players to build the power needed for serves and groundstrokes.

Integrating these components into a comprehensive training plan improves overall performance, guiding players on a consistent journey to achieve their maximum potential.

Transitioning from mastering English and tennis involves a mix of commitment, skill improvement, and organized training. By understanding the distinction between talent and potential and applying the ABCSS framework, aspiring tennis players can train with purpose and optimism. Embrace the process, remain dedicated, and allow your passion for the game to propel your growth. With commitment and a well-thought-out training regimen, reaching excellence is not merely achievable—it is guaranteed. Each effort you invest contributes to the distinct narrative of your athletic journey

Game Development.

In competitive tennis, moving from an aspiring player to a high-performance athlete relies on strategic training and focused game development. For players showing potential, it is crucial to implement a coaching plan that refines their technical abilities while enhancing their mental and emotional strengths. By concentrating on the five essential game situations that characterize tennis singles, coaches can establish a structured and intentional training environment.

The Five Game Situations.

Tennis singles is a complex sport that requires a wide range of skills. To succeed, players need to be proficient in five key game scenarios, each calling for specific technical and movement abilities. Grasping these scenarios is fundamental to performance coaching and crucial for enhancing a player's competitive capabilities.

1. Serving.

Serving goes beyond just initiating each point; it's a strategic tool that can control the game's momentum. An effective serve blends strength and accuracy, targeting spots that limit the opponent's choices. Coaches ought to stress:

Method: Emphasize grip, posture, and swinging technique.

Introduce a range of serve types, including flat, slice, and kick serves.

Encourage players to practice placing their serves in various areas of the service box.

2. Receiving.

Receiving serves is just as vital to a player's performance. Skillful receiving establishes the foundation for the following rally, so players need to create strategies to effectively respond to their opponents' serves. Important elements to focus on include:

Anticipation: Instruct players to interpret the server's body language and racket positioning.

Footwork: Enhance swift side-to-side movements and powerful starts to respond effectively to different types of serves.

Return Variety: Employ both bold returns and cautious placements depending on the context.

3. Rallying from the Baseline.

Baseline rallies are fundamental to many matches, as players compete in a test of endurance, placement, and strategy. To succeed in this scenario:

Consistency: Guide players to develop a reliable rallying stroke that focuses on depth and spin.

Shot Selection: Foster tactical awareness to choose the appropriate shot according to the opponent's positioning and habits.

Incorporate exercises that focus on side-to-side movement and pivoting to ensure stability during extended rallies.

Approaching the Net to Perform a Volley.

Transitioning from the baseline to the net is a crucial tactic for finishing points effectively. A strong net game enhances a player's overall arsenal and can surprise opponents during matches. To enhance this skill:

Approach Shots: Focus on developing approach shots that create opportunities for a volley.

Volleys: Train players in various volley techniques, including forehand, backhand, and overhead volleys.

Net Coverage: Emphasize positioning and footwork to enable quick responses to the opponent's returns.

5. Playing Against an Opponent Approaching the Net

Confronting an opponent at the net poses a distinct challenge, requiring players to guard against fierce volleys and predict their rival's actions. Important tactics to consider are:

Passing Shots: Instruct players to cultivate precise and strong passing shots.

Use lobs as a defensive tactic to counter an opponent's position at the net.

Encourage players to employ feints and body language to confuse their opponents, generating opportunities for effective plays.

Performance coaching in tennis involves a dynamic balance of improving technical abilities and building mental strength. Focusing training on five key game situations—serving, receiving, baseline rallies, net approaches, and countering net play—enables coaches to provide players with essential tools to enhance their game. With a deliberate and organized training strategy, aspiring tennis players can achieve their maximum potential, not just as athletes, but as strategic competitor's adept at handling the challenges of performance tennis.

Technical Development.

Tennis is a sport that goes beyond just physical capability; it combines mental sharpness, emotional strength, and outstanding technical skills. We will now offer a comprehensive insight into the training methods crucial for cultivating a tennis player, emphasizing the collaboration between coaches and players, the importance of technical growth, and the mental tactics that can improve performance.

The Connected Functions of Coach and Learner.

In tennis, the cooperative dynamic between coach and player is essential for achieving success. This relationship goes beyond a simple transaction; it is a shared journey toward excellence. Coaches provide knowledge and skill development, while players actively engage in their growth. Together, they establish a focused learning space where feedback is prompt and practical.

As training commences, it's essential to engage in each session with a clear purpose. This includes establishing precise goals, whether aimed at learning a new technique or enhancing a current skill. Both individuals involved need to share a mutual understanding of these objectives to ensure each training session is as effective as possible.

The Learning Environment: Transitioning from Closed to Open Situations.

The progression of technical skill development in tennis can be clearly demonstrated by moving from closed to open training scenarios. In the early stages, players train in a controlled environment where variables are limited. This enables them to concentrate entirely on perfecting specific techniques without the distractions found in competitive situations.

Skill Development is Closed.

In closed skill development, players perform individual drill exercises. They might work on their serves in isolation, concentrating on grip, stance, and follow-through. This setting enables precise improvement of every aspect of the shot. The coach can offer instant feedback, correct technique, and build the student's confidence.

Semi-Open Scenarios: Game Simulation Exercises.

After achieving comfort and proficiency, the next phase involves semi-open scenarios that incorporate game-like drills. These drills mimic match conditions while maintaining some control. For instance, two players might engage in rallying drills where one acts as an opponent, allowing for predetermined responses.

This phase is essential for utilizing technical skills in a more dynamic environment, promoting adaptability. Players start to understand how to respond to various shot types and angles while keeping their technical focus intact. The coach's feedback during these sessions remains critical, as it aids players in adjusting their techniques on the spot.

Move to Open Scenarios: Competitive Gameplay.

The last stage of the learning process involves moving to completely open situations, represented by competitive play. In this setting, players are required to regularly utilize their technical skills while under pressure, merging their training with actual matches. They need to adapt their strategies based on their opponents and the different dynamics of the game.

At this point, engaging with competition strengthens the player's abilities and challenges their mental resilience. This environment allows experience to shine and adaptability to become crucial. The coach's role shifts to one of observing, analyzing, and providing strategic advice, aiding players in discovering their flow in a high-pressure setting. To attain success in performance tennis, players must diligently refine a range of technical skills. The essential elements consist of:

Technical Skills: The Essential Elements.

Mastering the serve is essential because it establishes the foundation for the point; it is the only shot that a player can fully control. A player's skill in handling serves can influence the dynamics of a match.

Rallying: Building consistency in groundstrokes enables players to participate in extended rallies, gradually exhausting their opponents.

Approaching the Net: Moving toward the net from the baseline requires a unique set of skills and strategies that can be beneficial.

Net Play: Successfully performing volleys and overheads demands accuracy and rapid reflexes. Every one of these technical skills demands dedicated practice and is regularly reviewed during a player's training.

The Importance of Mindset and Breathing Methods.

Technical skills are fundamental to tennis performance, but developing the right mindset is just as important. A player's mental condition frequently determines their ability to perform skills effectively under pressure. Methods like visualization, where athletes picture themselves executing successful plays, can enhance confidence and mental toughness.

Breathing techniques are essential for managing anxiety and improving concentration. When athletes master their breathing, they can control their heart rate and stay calm in stressful moments. Adding mindfulness practices to their training can greatly enhance the mental environment for players, enabling them to perform at their best.

Tennis is not merely a goal but an ongoing journey of constant growth. The combination of technical abilities and a positive mindset, along with the support of a dedicated coach, forms a strong foundation for training. By recognizing the shift from closed to open skill scenarios and using effective mental strategies, players can enhance their performance significantly. Embrace the journey; each stroke, rally, and match contribute to the infinite quest for excellence on the court.

Competitive development: Tactical development.

Tennis is more than just a physical game; it is a strategic battle that unfolds on the court. For players with potential, developing competitive skills is crucial in their quest for improvement. We will now delve into the nuances of tactical skill development, emphasizing the need for both mental and emotional growth alongside physical training.

Understanding Tactical Development.

Tactical skill development in tennis is not a one-size-fits-all approach. It requires an intersection of experience, mental acuity, emotional resilience, and social understanding. As players advance, they must work on developing their tactical IQ, which encompasses their ability to analyse matches, adjust strategies on the fly, and make smart decisions under pressure.

The Relationship between Skills and Development.

Technical Skills and Physical Development: Technical skills are influenced by a player's physical abilities. Young or physically developing athletes may require a different focus than seasoned players. Ensuring that technique is anchored in good body mechanics will lead to better outcomes on the court.

Tactical Skills and Mental/Emotional Development: Tactical development is closely tied to the mental, emotional, and social development of the player. Younger players or those newer to competition may struggle with tension, focus, and the social dynamics of competitive play. Thus, integrating mental training sessions—focusing on visualization, concentration, and emotional regulation—into practice can enhance strategic capabilities.

Basic Tactics of Tennis.

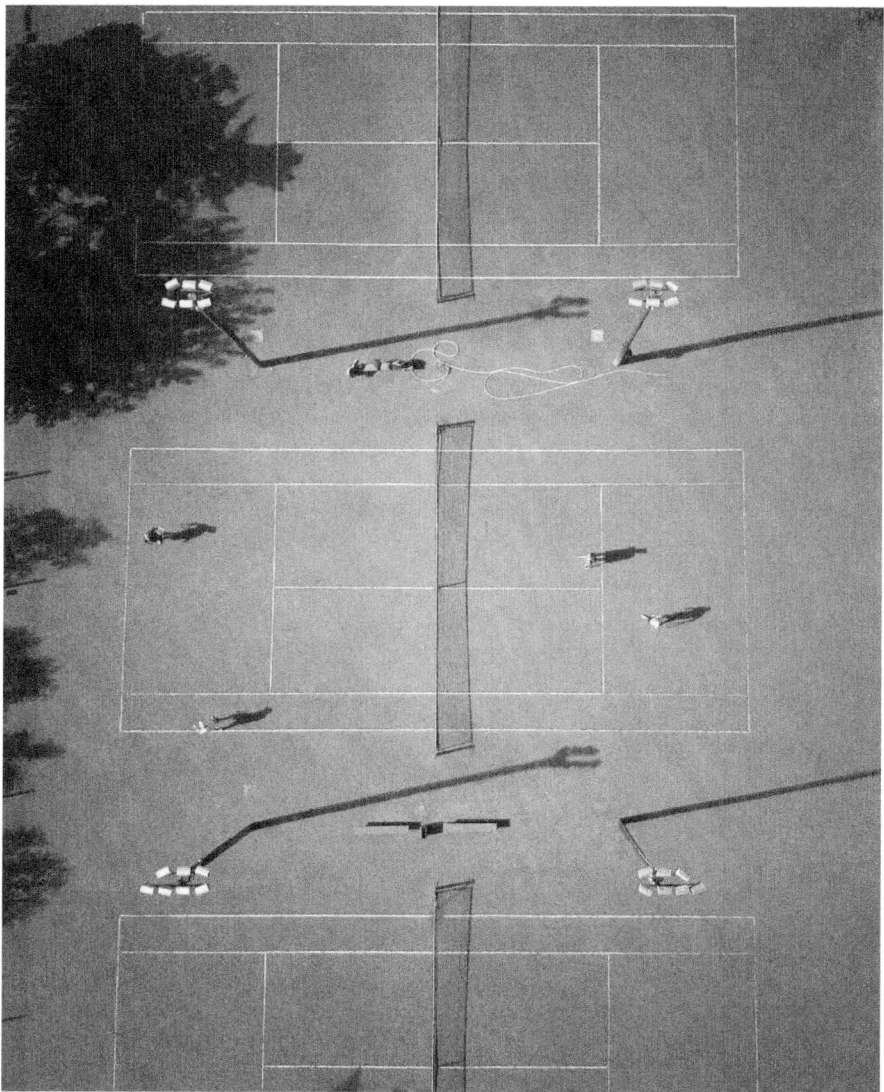

To develop competitive players, it is essential to instill an understanding of fundamental tactics that will guide their on-court decisions. Below are the five basic tactics every player should master:

1. Get the Ball Over the Net and Into the Court: Be Consistent.

Consistency is the foundation of successful tennis. Players must prioritize keeping the ball in play. By focusing on consistent strokes, they will learn to develop their rhythm and timing, allowing them to transition into more complex strategies.

Drills: Implement target practice drills focusing on hitting specific areas of the court consistently.

Mindset: Encourage players to adopt a growth mindset, understanding that every shot is an opportunity for improvement.

2. Hit the Ball to a Place that Makes it More Difficult for the Opponent to Hit it Back: Be Accurate.

Accuracy can tilt the match in a player's favor. Targeting areas of the court that are difficult for opponents to reach forces them into uncomfortable positions, often leading to errors.

Observation: Teach players to observe their opponents' positioning and anticipate their weaknesses.

Practice: Use cone drills to improve target accuracy during rallies.

3. Keep a Good Position on the Court and Try to Move the Opponent into a Poor Position.

Court positioning and footwork are essential components of effective tennis play. Staying in an advantageous position allows players to exert pressure while forcing their opponents to chase balls.

Footwork Drills: Implement agility drills that focus on quick lateral movements and recovery positioning.

Simulation: Practice situational drills that encourage players to focus on maintaining optimal court positioning.

4. Do What You Do Best More Often: Play to Your Strengths.

Every player has unique strengths, whether it's a powerful serve, a strong forehand, or exceptional volleying skills. Recognizing and utilizing these strengths is vital for competitive success.

Self-Scouting: Encourage players to conduct a self-assessment to identify their strengths and weaknesses.

Strategic Play: Develop match strategies that allow players to leverage their strengths in critical points of a match.

5. Determine the Opponent's Challenges: Exploit Their Weaknesses.

Recognizing and taking advantage of an opponent's vulnerabilities frequently determines the outcome of a match. Players need to develop the skill to spot patterns and flaws in their adversaries' gameplay.

Match Evaluation: Instruct players on identifying the weaknesses of opponents during practice games.

Encourage adaptability in tactics. If the initial strategies are not effective, players should be prepared to make necessary adjustments.

Integrating tactical skill development into regular training sessions is crucial for the advancement of competitive tennis players. Focusing on aspects such as consistency, accuracy, positioning, utilizing strengths, and taking advantage of opponents' weaknesses will boost players' competitive edge. Additionally, a comprehensive training strategy that encompasses mental and emotional growth will not only create skilled tennis players but also well-rounded competitors prepared to tackle the challenges of the sport effectively.

Comprehensive training and a dedication to strategic planning can help aspiring tennis players achieve their maximum potential, fostering ongoing development both on and off the court.

Cool Down.

As you approach the end of your performance session, ideally lasting about 2.5 hours, it's crucial to follow a comprehensive cool down routine. This phase not only aids in recovery but also sets the tone for your next training session. Below is a structured guide to ensure you maximize your cool down process effectively.

1. Assess your Position.

Take a moment to look back at what you've accomplished during your training. Ask yourself:

What drills or matches did I excel in?

Were there specific techniques that I found challenging?

How did I manage my time and energy on the court?

Reflection is key; understanding what worked well and where you need to improve allows you to tailor your future sessions accordingly.

2. Optimism and Inner Dialogue.

It's important to acknowledge your efforts, regardless of how the session panned out. Engage in positive self-talk by:

Listing three things you did well today.

Reminding yourself of your progress over the weeks.

Recognizing your commitment to improvement.

Cultivating a positive mindset boosts motivation and encourages you to keep pushing towards your goals.

3. Preparing for Upcoming Sessions.

Based on your evaluation, it's time to set the groundwork for your next training session. Outline:

Specific objectives for the upcoming week.

Areas that require extra focus.

Techniques that need further practice.

Creating a structured plan enhances goal-oriented training and helps maintain focus.

4.Connect with Other Players.

Open a dialogue with your fellow players about what they learned during the session. Questions may include:

What was your biggest takeaway?

Which aspects felt easier than before?

How do you feel about the match dynamics?

This peer interaction not only fosters a sense of community but also encourages shared learning experiences.

5. Hydration and Nutritional Support.

Recharging your body post-exercise is vital. Within 40 minutes of finishing your session, ensure you:

Re-hydrate: Drink water or an electrolyte drink to replenish lost fluids.

Snack wisely: Aim for a protein-rich snack (e.g., a protein bar, smoothie, or yogurt) to aid muscle recovery and sustain energy levels.

Effective nutrition post-training plays a significant role in your overall performance and readiness for future sessions.

6. Flexibility and Safety Through Stretching.

To conclude your cool down, static stretching is crucial. It helps with muscle recovery and greatly lowers the chances of injuries. Include these stretches:

Hamstring Stretch: Sit on the ground with one leg extended and reach towards your toe.

Quadriceps Stretch: Stand and pull your heel towards your glutes, holding onto a wall for balance.

Shoulder Stretch: Bring one arm across your body, using the other arm to press it towards your chest.

Calf Stretch: Stand facing a wall, place one foot back and lean against the wall to stretch the calf.

Hold each stretch for 15-30 seconds, breathing deeply and allowing your body to relax.

The Significance of Cooling Down.

A well-organized cool down routine is essential for enhancing your athletic performance and development. By assessing your workout, maintaining a positive mindset, preparing for future sessions, building relationships with teammates, focusing on nutrition, and including proper stretching, you create a pathway for both quick recovery and sustained success on the court. Always keep in mind: the conclusion of one session lays the groundwork for the next.

Section Four: Short Story.
The Last Serve: A Lesson in Life and Tennis.

In the small town of Zahora on the beautiful Costa de La Luz in the Cadiz province of Andalusia, nestled within the sun-kissed embrace of the southern Spanish Atlantic coast, lies the enchanting Playa de Faro Trafalgar. Here, the rhythm of the wave's dances against the golden sands, creating a symphony of sound that resonates with the heartbeats of locals and travellers alike. The air, rich with the scent of salt and wild herbs, carries whispers of stories woven through time, echoing the presence of ancient mariners who once sought safe passage guided by the steadfast lighthouse that stands sentinel over the coast. Just a few steps from the soft, warm grains of the beach, there exists a modest tennis club Corden Tennis & English Academy, a haven of determination and camaraderie. The sounds of rackets striking balls punctuate the air, melding seamlessly with the distant lapping of the waves. Students laugh and cheer as they embrace the joy of the game, this humble arena, with its sun-bleached nets and clay-coloured courts, serves as a crucible for dreams—where aspiring athletes sculpt their futures with every swing.

At the centre of this vibrant commotion stands Victor Acevedo, a wise and hopeful tennis coach revered in the community. With his tanned skin and gentle smile, he embodies the spirit of Zahora—a blend of warmth and resilience. His passion for the game transcends far beyond technique; he nurtures both skill and character, understanding that the essence of every player extends far beyond the court. Surrounding the club, native trees create a natural sanctuary that enchants all who pass. Gnarled olive trees, their ancient trunks twisted with the wisdom of centuries, stand watch over the courts, offering a whisper of shade and serenity. Beyond them, clusters of wild rosemary release their fragrant oils with every gentle breeze, infusing the air with a soothing aroma that calms the soul. The resilient stone pines, with their towering heights and sprawling branches, create a sense of shelter, as if nature itself has wrapped its arms around this community of aspiring champions.

As the sun begins its descent towards the horizon, a magical quality envelops the Playa de Faro Trafalgar. The light dances on the waves, turning them into a shimmering blanket of liquid gold. Surfers, silhouetted against the fiery sky, ride the rolling surf with daring grace, embodying the spirit of adventure that the beach inspires. Victor gathers his young players at the edge of the beach, forming a circle as the waves crash gently at their feet. Together, they share stories of resilience, determination, and the dreams that propel them forward. The ocean, a vast metaphor for life, serves as a backdrop to their aspirations. Victor encourages them to embrace the challenges they face, just as the waves embrace the shore, finding beauty even in the tumult of life's struggles. As twilight falls, the netting of the tennis courts casts delicate shadows on the earth, and the stars begin to twinkle above, representing the infinite possibilities that lie ahead. Each player leaves not only with the echoes of Victor's teachings but also with the spark of inspiration ignited by their time at the coast—woven from the fabric of community, nature, and dreams realized.

In this corner of Zahora, where the Playa de Faro Trafalgar meets the Atlantic coast, the essence of life unfolds in layers. This is a place where tennis serves as a powerful metaphor for growth, resilience, and the endless pursuit of excellence. The club, the trees, and the waves come together to create a nurturing environment that fosters champions not only on the court but in the game of life. Here, dreams are not merely born; they are cultivated, nourished by the passion and wisdom of a coach who believes in the transformative power of both sport and community.

With fluid strokes that seemed to echo the grace of a dancer, Lily poured her heart into the game, her tennis strokes shimmering with promise. The court was her stage, a canvas where she painted her aspirations with each serve and volley. Yet, underneath her fierce determination lay the uncertainty of youth—the fear of failure, the invisible shackles of doubt that tethered her progress. To the outside observer, Lily was a whirlwind of energy, a tempest on the court. Her movements were sharp and precise, the way she split stepped around the lines reminiscent of true athletic performance. Eyes bright with ambition, she embodied the spirit of competitiveness. But beneath that vibrant exterior, in the quiet moments of solitude, a different reality would unfold. Sitting alone on the cracks of the old tennis court, as the day began to fade into twilight, Lily was grappled by an unsettling feeling.

The whispers of inadequacy crept into her consciousness, sowing seeds of doubt that sprouted like weeds in her mind. What if she wasn't good enough? What if, at the crucial moment, her mind betrayed her? These questions haunted her during every match, a spectral presence, lurking just beyond her peripheral vision. It was like trying to catch a shadow—elusive, always just out of reach. The thrill of victory was often overshadowed by the fear of defeat, leaving her in a constant tug-of-war with her own expectations.

One warm afternoon, as the sun painted the sky in hues of orange and pink, Lily found herself alone at the court, practicing her serves. The sound of the ball striking her racket echoed in the stillness, each thwack a declaration to the world: "I am here." With every serve, she began to shed layers of her apprehension, her focus sharpening with each repetition. The rhythmic motion of her body brought a sense of freedom, the swirling doubts fading into the background like distant thunder. Breath by breath, she discovered the joy within the struggle, the beauty that lay in persistence. With every successful serve, she felt a little lighter, a little more confident.

Lily realized that perfection was an illusion, a mirage demanding too high a price. It was an understanding that each hit wasn't just about winning or losing but a lesson ingrained in every repetition. The beauty of the game, much like life, resided in its imperfections. It thrived on unpredictability, on the unexpected turns that kept players on their toes. Embracing her flaws became a new weapon in her arsenal. The fear of failure transformed into a drive for improvement. Each missed shot was no longer a mark of shame but a stepping stone towards growth. Guided by the newfound clarity of her heart, Lily began to reframe her journey—a journey not only of athletic prowess but of self-discovery and resilience. As the evening light, Lily took a step back, resting her racket against the net. The doubts that had once loomed like storm clouds were now nothing more than fleeting thoughts, dissipating into the darkening sky.

She understood that the game mirrored life; it was not about avoiding failure but learning to rise after every fall. In that serene moment, with the horizon glowing in the twilight, Lily felt a profound sense of peace envelop her. She wasn't just fighting against her fears; she was learning to dance with them, to make them a part of her story. She would carry this lesson with her—not just on the court but wherever life led her next. And with that, Lily left the court, not just a player, but a warrior in her own right, ready to embrace every challenge that lay ahead.

Yet, one misplaced shot sent the ball spiralling into the nearby sand dunes on Zahora Beach—a symbol of her frustrations. She slumped to the ground, staring at her trembling hands, a tempest of emotions brewing inside her. Victor, who had been observing from a distance, approached her quietly, his presence soothing like a gentle breeze. He sat down beside her, allowing a silence to wrap around them like a warm blanket. The rhythmic sound of the waves greeted their ears, a soft lullaby amidst the chaos of her thoughts. "Lily," he began thoughtfully, "do you see the sea?" He pointed towards the shimmering waters, which mirrored the sky's brilliant colours. "It is calm today, but storms will come—waves crashing, winds howling.

The true beauty of the sea lies not in its stillness but in its ability to embrace the storm and return to serenity." Lily looked at him, puzzled. She had always viewed the ocean as a backdrop to her struggles, a place for escape rather than reflection. Victor continued, "Life, much like tennis, is not just about winning. It's about how you face the challenges. Each mistake is a chance to learn, to grow." She shifted, her gaze drifting back to the dunes where her ball lay, half-buried in the sand like her confidence. "But sometimes, it feels like I keep making the same mistakes. I should be better than this." Victor smiled gently. "That's precisely it. The great players embody resilience. They don't dwell on a setback. They analyse, adapt, and keep moving forward. Think about your last match. Remember when you misjudged that serve? It led you to adjust your footing. You learned, didn't you?" "Yes, but it still hurts," she admitted, frustration leaking into her voice. "Of course it does. Emotions are vital; they deepen our experiences. But don't let them anchor you. Instead, let them be the tide that teaches you to rise." Victor leaned back on the sand, letting the grains slip through his fingers. "How many times have you witnessed the tide retreating only to return stronger? That's how life works, Lily. You face setbacks, but they shape you." Looking out at the ocean, she began to see what he meant.

The water ebbed and flowed, both serene and tumultuous, yet always moving forward. "So you're saying that every time I struggle, it's just a part of my journey?" "Exactly. Each match is an opportunity—every point a lesson. Look at your wins; notice how they were born from learning. You have faced lockets of failure to shine in your triumphs." Victor pushed himself to stand, extending a hand towards her. "Stand up," he urged. "How will you face the next serve if you remain down here? Just as the waves never hesitate to rise again, neither should you." Slowly, Lily accepted his hand, feeling his strength pull her up against the gentle resistance of the sand. She followed Victor's gaze back to the sea, taking a deep breath, inhaling the salty air mingled with the scent of possibility. "Let's try again. Let the waves be your guide," he said. They turned back towards the net, leaving behind the sand dunes. Each step felt lighter, every heartbeat more resolute. As she prepared for another serve, the horizon stretched wide before her—the vast expanse of opportunity ready to be explored. Once more, she gripped her racket, but this time, instead of fear, she welcomed the challenge. One serve at a time.

The waves of past errors reminded her of the tides, but today, she would ride the waves toward the shore of growth. "Ready?" Victor called, a smile brightening his face. "With you by my side," she answered, "I think I'm ready." The spark within her—a reminder that life, like tennis, is not merely about the victory, but the journey and the lessons learned along the way.

Weeks turned into months, and as the club prepared for the prestigious Zahora Open, Lily trained with renewed fervour. Each dawn found her on the court, racket in hand, pushing beyond her previous limits. She embraced each drill and practice session, turning her frustrations into fuel. With every swing of her racket, she infused her movements with purpose, transforming what once felt heavy into a dance of resilience and dynamism. The rhythm of her footsteps, combined with the sharp crack of the ball hitting the strings, became a symphony of growth, resonating with her heart's newfound beat. In this whirlwind of training, she learned to embrace the unpredictability of the game. The swirling winds of fate no longer seemed like roadblocks; instead, they became winds guiding her through uncertainty. She carved her path through doubt and fear like a sculptor chiselling a perfect piece of art from a block of marble.

Each practice match was not just a rehearsal for the big tournament but an exploration of her inner strength and an affirmation of her tenacity. On the day of the tournament, the stands were packed, eager spectators filling every crevice of the sunlit court. The atmosphere buzzed with excitement, and Lily's heart raced—not from anxiety, but from a deep-seated thrill. The cheers of the crowd enveloped her like a warm embrace, amplifying her spirit. She took a moment to breathe, letting gratitude wash over her. Here she was, an embodiment of resilience forged in the heat of trials, against a backdrop of whispers and applause that felt both foreign and familiar. As she stepped onto the court, the chill of the moment struck her like a wave, but with it came clarity. This was her stage, her arena—her opportunity to showcase the transformation she had undergone.

The soft thud of her shoes against the court brought her focus to the present; she was alive in this moment, connected to everyone and everything around her. The first serve sailed over the net, slicing through the air with precision. She felt the rush of adrenaline surge through her veins. With each point played, she was being propelled by something deeper than just a desire to win. Each rally was an exchange, a conversation between her and her opponent. Every time the ball bounced back, she felt the lesson reaffirm itself—this game mirrored life, filled with unexpected turns and opportunities for growth. Through laughter and heartache, victory and defeat, Lily had embraced the essence of playing the game. As the final point approached, she felt an overwhelming sense of peace wash over her. Win or lose, she had won the most significant match of all—the one against her old self. The storm was no longer an enemy; it was a trusted ally on her journey, and as she prepared to unleash her final shot, she smiled, knowing whatever happened next would be part of her beautiful, chaotic story.

As her name echoed through the crowd, Lily stepped forward, heart pounding in her chest. The stadium shimmered with a sea of eager faces, each pair of eyes locked onto her as if the fate of the universe rested heavily on her shoulders. Surrounded by the weight of expectations, the ghost of doubt crept into her mind once more, whispering fears that she had tried so hard to silence. But as she glanced over to Victor, who stood at the edge of the court, his face a mask of unwavering faith, she felt the nervous whirlpool dissolve into a quiet resolve. There he was, her rock, her mentor, the voice of reason in the storm of her thoughts. The way he nodded, encouraging, solidified her determination; she would not let the moment define her; rather, she would define the moment.

The match began, tension crackling in the air like electricity. With each serve, Lily felt as though she was engaging in a sacred dialogue—an exchange between her and the universe. The very first ball was struck, and the sound resonated through the arena. As she watched it sail over the net, she was acutely aware of its trajectory and what her next moves needed to be. At first, the rallies flowed seamlessly, with a rhythm that echoed the heartbeat of the crowd. But as the first set progressed, she faltered. A missed backhand here, a distracted moment there, as if the ghosts of her past mistakes had come back to haunt her. The fear that accompanied each error clawed at her confidence, a nagging reminder of every time she had fallen short of her aspirations. Yet, she also soared. Moments of brilliance emerged like bright stars in a night full of doubts. She recalled the lake, where endless hours had been spent practicing her strokes, perfecting her serve.

The storms that had often disrupted her training, the clashes with the wind and rain that had mirrored her inner turmoil. Each experience had moulded her. And the calm that followed the storms—it was precisely that tranquillity she sought now, the focus that allowed her to push beyond her initial fears. With every point, she wrestled not just with her opponent but with the very essence of her existence. Was she here to win, or was she here to learn? Each game became a lesson, and each lesson a step further into understanding the importance of the journey over the destination.

The struggle transformed—no longer a burden but a part of her growth. She could hear Victor's voice in her mind, reminding her to breathe, to trust her instincts. In this moment, she was not just a competitor; she was a student of the game and of life itself. The beat of the crowd faded to a distant hum as her focus sharpened, allowing her to embrace both the challenge before her and the support that enveloped her from those who believed in her. As the final points of the match loomed closer, she felt a wave of calm wash over her. It was in that liberation from expectation that she found her strength. The net became less a barrier and more a bridge to the next step of her journey. Every serve was a testament to her resilience; every return, an affirmation of her commitment. In those fleeting moments, time stretched, and she became one with the court and the ethereal dance of the game. Winning or losing blurred into the background as she immersed herself in the beauty of the sport.

As the match neared its climax, she prepared herself for one last, decisive serve. The world held its breath, suspended in anticipation. She gathered her strength, her past experiences swirling together like a vivid tapestry, and with one swift motion, she struck the ball—a culmination of every lesson learned and every moment embraced. As it sailed over the net, she realized it wasn't just a point; it was the culmination of her journey. Regardless of the outcome, she had stepped beyond the shadows of doubt and into the light of her potential. Somewhere, amidst the noise and excitement, she had finally found her peace.

In those fleeting moments of triumph and despair, she discovered the core of her own strength. The crowd held its breath, a palpable tension hanging in the air as all eyes were fixed on Lily. She stood at the baseline, her heart pounding in sync with the rhythm of the game. The final serve loomed before her—not just a moment on the court, but a defining moment in her life. Memories flashed through her mind, each a shot in the tapestry of her journey. The countless early mornings spent practicing, the struggles of overcoming self-doubt, and the nagging injuries that had almost convinced her to give up. But here she was, on the verge of something greater. She felt the grip of her racket, the familiar weight comforting, grounding her amidst the whirlwind of emotions. With a deep breath, she prepared to serve. Her coach's voice echoed in her ears: "Believe in yourself, Lily. Trust your training." The words ignited a fire within her. This wasn't just a serve; it was a testament to her resilience.

With determination that seemed to transcend the confines of the court, she visualized the ball arcing perfectly over the net, spiralling toward destiny. The ball soared through the air, a blur of neon yellow against the deep blue sky. Time appeared to stand still, elongating the seconds as it travelled in what felt like slow motion. Would it land where she intended? The collective breath of the spectators surged as one, a unified gasp of hope mingled with the twilight air. Thwack! The sound was explosive. The ball struck the serve box. The echo resonated like a heartbeat of hope across the silent crowd. In that singular moment, with the crowd erupting into a symphony of cheers, she understood that life—much like tennis—is not defined solely by victory or defeat. Rather, it is shaped by the lessons learned and the courage discovered within oneself. The jubilant cries of her supporters washed over her, but in her heart, she silently thanked every hardship that forged her into this moment. As she revelled in the joy of the achievement, Lily's eyes drifted to the holm oak trees that framed the court—silent sentinels to her journey. They had witnessed her tears, her laughter, her frustrations, and her victories. In their shade, she found solace and wisdom, learning from the seasons of change around her. Now, in the aftermath of that pivotal serve, a new chapter was unfurling—not just for Lily, but for every dreamer who dared to embrace the storm.

In that moment, surrounded by the native encina oak trees, cheers, and the weight of her dreams, the echoes of that heartbeat of hope reminded her—this was just the beginning.

The oak's steadfastness mirrored her resilience; the winds that coursed through the branches symbolized the challenges that would come, each gust a reminder of the strength she had discovered within herself. As she walked to the net, hand raised in acknowledgment of her opponent, another wave of understanding rolled over her. Whatever lay ahead—more matches, more challenges—she knew she possessed the tools to navigate through the highs and lows. With her heart full and her spirit ignited, Lily smiled, not just at the victory she had achieved, but at the journey that awaited her. Life was a match, vast and unpredictable. And she was ready, poised to seize every moment, savouring both the wins and the lessons that would shape her path ahead.

On the side-lines, a few years away from a glorious retirement, stood Javier Morales, a once-legendary tennis star whose name was whispered in reverence. The sun hung low in the sky, as the rhythmic sound of balls hitting racquets resonated in the air, each thwack echoing memories he could never quite shake. Javier's life had been a whirlwind of victories and endorsements, each tournament a stepping stone to his unassailable throne in the world of tennis. Crowds had roared his name, and sponsors had showered him with riches. Yet here he was, cloaked in the twilight of his career, contemplating the weight of his legacy.

The sheen had dulled—his once-adored name now draped in shadows that slipped quietly into the corners of his fame. As he stood there, he observed the young players training, their faces glowing with determination. They reminded him of himself, decades ago, eager and restless on that very same court, chasing a dream with voracious energy. He could hear the echoes of his younger self—the sweat-soaked shirts, the fierce intensity of practice, the relentless ambition that had propelled him through numerous gruelling matches. Those battles on the court had shaped him, taught him more than just the mechanics of the game. Each serve had its own lesson, each forehand a fleeting future. He recalled a match at the peak of his career—a championship finale that had come down to the last set. The thrill of that moment, the pressure of the stands, the palpable tension in the air; it had been both exhilarating and suffocating.

In that moment of reflection, he remembered the advice of his coach, a wise old man whose face had aged like the leather of a well-worn racquet: "Winning isn't everything, Javier. It's about how you carry yourself when you lose." With the title clutched tightly in his grasp, Javier had felt invincible. Yet, as time slipped through his fingers, he began to understand the essence of that lesson. His legacy wasn't just about trophies or accolades; it was about the lives he touched and the values he imparted. It was about resilience, respect, and the relentless pursuit of excellence—not for the glory, but for the sheer love of the game. He glanced at the court where the new generation practiced their swings, fighting to carve their own stories. Their energy was intoxicating, yet it reminded him of the fragility of success. "What will they learn from me?" he pondered. With each strike of the ball, he felt the weight of his experiences—the failures, the regrets, but also the triumphs that had filled the tapestry of his life. Suddenly, an unexpected urge surged within him. It was time to share.

Time to reach beyond the polished walls of his accomplishments and guide those who stood where he once had. He approached the young players, each of them bubbling with potential yet cloaked in self-doubt and ambition. "Hey, can I share a few tips?" he ventured, his voice steady. They paused, their attention shifting from the ball to the man whose shoes they aspired to fill. As they gathered around him, their eyes wide with curiosity, Javier began to speak. The lessons that flowed from his heart were about more than tennis—they were about life. He spoke of perseverance, the importance of humility, and the value of community.

He shared stories of improbable victories, but also of heart-wrenching losses, each moment teaching him resilience in the face of adversity. In those moments, as he connected with the next generation, he felt a warmth blossoming inside—a realization that this was his true legacy. Perhaps retirement wasn't the end, but a beginning of sorts. An opportunity to mould young minds; to inspire them to rise, not just as champions on the court but as leaders in life. The sun dipped lower, painting the world in shades of orange and crimson. Javier Morales stood among the laughter and determination of youth, no longer just a fading star, but a guiding light. Through the lessons he imparted, he began to understand that in sharing his past, he was securing a future—both for himself and those who dared to dream. In the moments that followed, the court buzzed not just with the sound of tennis balls, but with the heartbeat of a new generation, fuelled by the lessons of a legend who had learned that true greatness isn't measured by victories, but by the lives you touch along the way.

Lily approached him cautiously, her feet quickening on the ground as she drew closer. There was an inquisitive spark in her gaze, mixing with a vibrant energy that reminded him of his own youth. "What's your greatest lesson in tennis?" she asked, her voice steady and filled with the kind of awe reserved for heroes. Javier chuckled softly, shaking the weight of nostalgia from his shoulders. The question hung in the air, stirring memories long forgotten. He looked down at her earnest expression, eyes wide with admiration like a sponge ready to soak up wisdom. "Tennis taught me that the match isn't won with power, but with heart," he replied, his voice deepening with reflection. He could see her processing his words, her youthful mind working to understand the deeper meaning hidden within the game they both loved. "Heart?" she echoed, tilting her head, curiosity piquing. "Yes," he said, leaning forward slightly, "It's about resilience and the will to persevere. You can hit the ball harder than anyone, but if you don't love what you're doing, if you don't truly invest yourself in each match, the wins will feel empty. You won't remember them." Lily nodded, a frown of concentration forming on her brow. "But what if you lose?" "Ah, losing is part of it." Javier replied, smiling gently. "Every great player has faced defeat. I remember a match early in my career—one that I thought I'd win easily. I was cocky. I lost in straight sets, but that taught me humility.

The sun glinted off the freshly chalked lines, the scent of newly cut grass mingling with the distant echo of tennis shoes sliding across the court. Each thud of a ball brought him back to a time when he too had been fearless. Javier had once wielded his racket like a sword, slashing through challenges with youthful exuberance—and yet, here he was, seated on the side-lines, watching a new generation ignite their passion for the game. His knees creaked as he shifted, and he felt the weight of the years pressing down on him. Each wrinkle on his face was a testament to both triumph and failure, the wins and losses woven into his very being. But today, as he watched the sunlight dance on the court, something stirred inside him—a flicker of the young man he used to be. It was during a particularly bright afternoon, framed by the laughter of players and the rhythmic bounce of tennis balls, that their paths crossed.

It opened my eyes; it reminded me that every opponent has something to teach you. You learn more from your failures than you do from your victories." Lily's eyes lit up with recognition, the pieces falling into place. "So, it's kind of like life?" she pondered aloud, her thoughts weaving the lessons of the court into the fabric of her existence. "Exactly," he said, feeling the warmth of camaraderie seep into the air. "Tennis is a microcosm of life. Every serve, every rally, it's all about handling pressure, about embracing the moment, both good and bad. It's about finding joy in the struggle." As they spoke, the sounds of the court faded into the background, the world around them blurring into insignificance. Javier saw in Lily a reflection of his younger self— her enthusiasm, so unfiltered and real. In that moment, he felt a renewed sense of purpose, as if he were passing a torch to her, igniting a fire that might someday burn just as fiercely. Lily grinned, her confidence growing, ready to step onto the court with newfound inspiration. "Thanks, coach Javier," she said, and with that, she dashed off to join her friends. Watching her retreat into the chaos of youthful exuberance, Javier felt a lightness in his heart. He may have left the court, but through her, he could still play, still teach, still inspire. And in that shared moment of honesty, he discovered that the greatest lessons are often passed on in the unlikeliest of encounters, reverberating through generations, matched only by the heartbeat of the game.

He watched as Francis missed a serve, the ball sailing wide and leaving the young player visibly frustrated. Lily's brow creased in confusion as she observed the impact of this moment. "See there?" Javier pointed out. "In that split second, he has a choice. He can either let that mistake take root in his mind, or he can rise above it, dust himself off, and continue." Lily nodded but still looked uncertain. "But why is the heart so important? I thought it was all about practice and skill." "In many ways, it is," Javier said, a hint of nostalgia colouring his voice. "But life isn't just about perfect strokes or flawless technique. It's about resilience, determination, and the ability to face disappointment without losing hope. In the end, it's not just about winning —it's about how you handle the loss." He felt a pang of nostalgia wash over him as he recalled the final sets of his own career. The aching defeats that had stung his pride lingered like shadows at the back of his mind. Each loss in his sports journey was akin to a fierce storm; it felt relentless, and each bruise seemed to knock the wind from his sails. Yet with each setback came a wealth of lessons learned, lessons that had shaped him both as a player and as a person. "Tell me," he continued, turning his gaze back to Francis. "What happens if he loses a match? What will he learn from it?" "Um, that he should practice more?" Lily ventured hesitantly. "Perhaps," Javier nodded, "but it's more than just physical improvement.

He gestured toward the court, where Francis, a promising young player, was demonstrating a serve technique. "Look at him—he has talent, sure, but does he have the heart?" The young player, Lily, followed his gaze, her eyes widening as Francis launched serve after serve, the crisp sound of the ball meeting the racket resonating in the stillness of the afternoon air. Each stroke seemed to echo with potential, yet Javier's words weighed on her mind like a persistent cloud. "What do you mean?" Lily asked, her curiosity piqued as she could easily see the young player's raw skill on display. "Isn't talent enough?" Javier chuckled softly, shaking his head as he motioned for Lila to sit beside him on the wooden bench that overlooked the court. "Talent can get you so far, but it's the heart that keeps you going when the chips are down," he explained.

He must understand that losing is an opportunity for growth. Each defeat is a chance to reflect, to adjust, to emerge stronger. It's the moments spent in the shadows that forge a true champion. It builds character." "What if he gives up?" Lily asked. "What if he doesn't have the heart to keep fighting?" "That's the gamble," Javier replied, a serious glint in his eye. "Every player, every person, faces that moment. The question is whether they dig deep. The heart is what allows us to rise after the fall, to transform defeat into stepping stones. In tennis the greatest victories often stem from the darkest defeats." Lily watched as Francis missed another serve, but this time, he shook his head with determination rather than despair. He adjusted his stance, focusing intently. There was a flicker of something in his eyes—a fire fuelled by the knowledge that it wasn't the mistake that mattered, but how he responded to it. Javier smiled, sensing Lila's understanding deepening. "Just Like that, " he said softly. "There's the heart."

Javier adjusted his grip on the racquet, feeling the familiar weight of it in his hand. Each stroke he'd ever taken, every match he'd fought, echoed in his memory, a chorus of triumphs and losses. Yet, today felt different. There was something about the air that was infused with a crispness that hinted at change. Victory had always been a fleeting ghost, a shimmering figure that danced just beyond reach. Each time he had tasted it—each tournament won, each cheer from the crowd—had been intoxicating. But those moments vanished like grains of sand slipping through his fingers, leaving behind an emptiness that felt heavier than the burdens of defeat. Defeat, on the other hand, was a companion he knew all too well. It wrapped around him like a leaden cloak, reminding him of his vulnerabilities, the times he had stumbled before an audience and the weight of hope that had crashed down upon him in the final point of a hard-fought match.

True strength, he had learned, wasn't in the overpowering of an opponent, but in the resilience it took to rise after every fall. Lily, his new protégé, stood beside him, her bright eyes brimming with excitement and curiosity. The innocence of youth shone through her expression as she watched him, hanging onto his every word. "But you won so many tournaments," she pressed, her voice bubbling with enthusiasm. "Doesn't that count as greatness?" Javier mused on her words, a smile flickering across his face as he conjured images of the trophies lined up on his mantle—gleaming testaments to his hard work and dedication. "Yes," he began slowly, his gaze drifting toward the horizon where the sun kissed the earth goodnight. "But what matters more is how we inspire others, how we carry our stories." He turned to face her fully, seeing not just a student but a reflection of his younger self—filled with hope, dreams, and the conviction that the world was theirs for the taking. "Every match is a chapter, Lily. And it's not the victories that are etched in history, but the lessons we carve from each stumble." She tilted her head, contemplating his words as if unravelling a puzzle. "So... losing is important too?" Javier nodded, his heart warming at her understanding. "Losing teaches us humility, patience, and perseverance. It's a reminder that the journey is just as significant as the destination. Each moment we spend rising from a fall shapes our character.

Greatness is not found in never losing; it's about how we grow in the aftermath." As they began to practice, Lily's relentless drive filled the air with a rhythm only a budding athlete could unleash. Each swing of her racquet was a manifestation of her dreams, and Javier admired the spark that ignited her spirit. They rallied back and forth, the ball a bright blur between them, echoing their laughter like a heartbeat syncing to the pulse of mentorship. In that exchange, he witnessed the beauty of it all: the playful competition, the spirit of togetherness, and the shared bond of a love for the game. Tennis, like life, thrived in moments of ebb and flow, of highs and lows, and of the courage required to embrace each moment with grace. "Remember, Lily," he called out as they paused for a drink break, "every match comes with its own set of lessons. Whether you win or lose, it's how you choose to rise that defines you. Carry that forward, and you will always find greatness within—or perhaps, far beyond the court." Javier hoped that in teaching her the game, he was also imparting the greatest lesson of all: the enduring power of resilience and the unbreakable spirit of hope.

He leaned slightly closer, the secrets of his heart spilling forth like a soft whisper. "Greatness is in the journey, in the connections we make, and in how we uplift those around us." Lily watched Francis sweat and strain, a picture of determination. His brow was furrowed, beads of sweat rolling down his forehead, glistening under the mid-afternoon sun like tiny jewels. She could see every muscle tense as he prepared for the next serve. "Do you think he'll make it?" she asked, an edge of concern in her voice, tinted with hope. "Maybe," Javier replied thoughtfully, his gaze fixed on the court, where Francis was locked in a fierce duel against one of his toughest opponents. "But it won't just depend on his serves or his swings. It will depend on how he learns to fight through his own battles—his perseverance when the game isn't going his way, his humility when he wins." Lily's brow furrowed as confusion painted her features. "So, you're saying it's about more than just the game?" "Exactly," Javier said, a quiet passion igniting in his voice. "Tennis isn't just about the score. It's about the lessons learned, the resilience forged in the heat of competition, and the character that shines through when the lights are brightest."

As Francis launched himself into another rally, the sound of the ball connecting with his racket echoed like a heartbeat—a rhythm that reminded Lily of the relentless nature of life. It was a dance, she thought, each movement calculated yet fluid, each decision a reflection of inner strength or a fleeting moment of fear. "Look at him go," she breathed, her eyes wide. "But—" "But?" Javier prompted, turning to meet her gaze. "There's so much pressure. What if he falters? What if this is the moment everything unravels?" The thoughts tumbled out of her, laced with anxiety. Pressure is a part of the game, and of life," Javier said, his voice steady. "What matters is not the stumbling but the getting up. Watch him. He's not just fighting against his opponent; he's battling the voices that tell him he can't. That's where the true win lies." The match wore on, and with each passing moment, Francis morphed into a master storyteller through his play—narrating a saga of triumph, doubt, and fortitude. With every point scored, the tension shifted; with every point lost, a new lesson unfurled. "See that?"

Javier pointed as Francis demonstrated brilliant footwork, sliding across the court with grace. "He's adapting. That's what life is—adapting to the challenges thrown your way." Lily nodded slowly, her heart swelling with admiration for Francis. He hadn't just trained his body for this moment; he had nurtured a mindset built on perseverance and resilience. In his struggles, she could see reflections of her own. As Francis won a particularly tense rally, the crowd erupted, and he raised his racket in triumph. In that moment, Lily felt an unexpected warmth, a realization igniting within her. She turned to Javier, her voice steadier now. "It's not about the destination, is it?" "No," he replied, a smile creeping onto his face. "It never has been. It's about who we become along the way. Every match, every setback, every little victory—it's all a brushstroke in the masterpiece of our lives.

" And as the final points unfolded on the court, Lily understood: in the intricate game of tennis—as in life—greatness was born not merely from winning, but from the unwavering spirit to rise, connect, and uplift those around us. With newfound clarity, she watched as Francis prepared for his final serve. Victory was still uncertain, but what resonated loud and clear was the certainty that greatness was rooted in the heart, not just the scoreboard. "Come on, Francis!" she cheered, the echoes of life lessons swirling around her—a potent reminder that every match, much like every moment, was an opportunity to strive for something greater, to be part of something bigger, and to uplift others along the way. In that instant, she realized that the beautiful game of tennis mirrored the beautiful journey of life—not just in wins or losses, but in the heart and soul of every player.

"Tennis, like life, is often about how gracefully we handle our victories and our defeats." The words hung in the air between them, punctuated by the soft thud of a tennis ball bouncing against the court. The gruelling afternoon light bathed the surroundings transforming the familiar practice courts into a vast arena of possibilities. Javier leaned against the weathered wooden fence, watching Lily as she approached the service line, her brow furrowed in concentration. She was a promising young player; her unyielding spirit reminded him of his own youth, filled with dreams and aspirations. As she stared at the ball perched precariously on her racket, he wondered if she understood the weight of both triumph and loss—the duality that shaped a person both on and off the court. Their conversation unfolded woven with laughter, wisdom, and understanding. Javier could feel a bond forming, one that transcended mere mentorship.

With every word exchanged, they were crafting not just a lesson about tennis, but a shared understanding about resilience. Javier felt a profound sense of solace wash over him. He gazed at Lily, who was nodding thoughtfully at his words. In this moment, he realized something monumental: maybe his greatest legacy wouldn't be his trophies—gleaming reminders of past glories—but the moments shared and the lessons imparted to the next generation of players. "Now, are you ready to try learning that serve?" he challenged playfully, a smile tugging at the corners of his mouth. Lily's eyes sparkled with enthusiasm, her nerves momentarily forgotten. "Ready as I'll ever be!" she exclaimed, mimicking his playful tone. There was a flicker of determination in her stance, the fire of ambition igniting a flame within her. Javier positioned himself next to her, offering gentle guidance as she prepared to serve. "Remember, it's not just about power; it's also about finesse," he instructed, watching her movements intently. "You want to place the ball where your opponent least expects it." With each attempt, they laughed together, sharing in the excitement of small victories—each successful serve, each perfect arc of the ball sailing over the net. But soon, frustration crept in when the ball didn't meet her expectations.

With a newfound determination, Lily nodded vigorously, stepping closer to the court. The air was electric, thick with the energy of dreams and aspirations, as competitors stretched and warmed up their muscles. Lily's heart raced with every beat, the rhythmic thud of the nearby practice courts echoing her own inner turmoil. Victor smiled from a distance, observing her with a knowing gaze. He had been her coach, mentor, and friend—a guiding light on her path to self-discovery. Today, however, he wondered if maybe, just maybe, this moment was bigger than tennis itself. It was about transformation, igniting passion not only within Lily but also in every player who graced the courts. The final serve wasn't merely a game; it was the embodiment of dreams waiting to be realized—the fragile yet unyielding spirit that connected each player.

He observed the way she bit her lip, pushing herself harder, just as he had done countless times before. "Lily," he called softly, drawing her attention away from the court. "What's most important is not how many times you miss, but how you recover from those misses. In life, just like in tennis, it's easy to get discouraged. But it's the ability to shake it off and try again that defines you." Her gaze softened, understanding washing over her features. "It's okay to mess up, then?" she asked, her voice tinged with vulnerability. "Absolutely," he affirmed with warmth. "Every great player has faced their own set of challenges. It's how they respond that makes the difference." With renewed determination, Lily approached the service line once more. As she tossed the ball into the air, this time there was a new light in her eyes— confidence laced with acceptance. The ball soared over the net, landing precisely where she had aimed. A triumphant grin spread across her face, and Javier felt a rush of pride swell within him. The court slowly faded into twilight, but the lessons of the day—the shared laughter, the whispers of wisdom—remained etched in the air, a timeless testament to the game of life and the artistry of tennis.

The day of the regional tournament arrived, a stage glittering with aspirations and dreams. Spectators filled the stands, their cheers blending into a cacophony of excitement. The smell of freshly cut grass mingled with the petrichor of previous rains—a reminder of nature's resilience. Here, on this vibrant canvas of clay and determination, every player cast their fears aside as the matches progressed, the weight of expectation loomed over Lily like a thundercloud. Each point won swelled her confidence, while points lost chipped away at her resolve. She found herself weaving in and out of memories of late-night practices, Javier's hauntingly beautiful words echoing in her ears: "Tennis is like life. It's about resilience, learning to stand tall after every fall." The gravity of those words grounded her. When it was finally her turn to step onto the court, she could hear Javier's voice in the background, encouraging yet calm. Each serve was like a heartbeat—timed and precise. With every stroke of her racket, she remembered not only how to win but also the importance of playing with heart. Her opponents blurred into shadows, figures representing obstacles she had faced in life—a demanding father, the struggle for acceptance, and the fear of failure.

Each game became a metaphor for overcoming the odds, and she began to realize that tennis wasn't merely about scoring points—it was about the journey itself. As the final game approached its climax, tension hung in the air. The crowd held its breath, collective pulses racing in sync with Lily's. With sweat trickling down her brow and the stakes higher than ever, she drew from the well of inspiration that had fuelled her journey. There was a moment—a heartbeat—where she was suspended in time. She thought of Victor's legacy, of the fire he had kindled in her spirit. With a fierce yell, she served—a powerful arching ball that soared through the air like an arrow. Everyone watched as it struck the court, the sound resonating like a victory bell. Cheers erupted, filling her ears with joyous noise, yet in that moment, she felt a profound silence. It was as if the universe was whispering, "This is your triumph, not because of the score, but because you dared to rise." As she wrapped her fingers around the trophy, it shimmered under the sunlight, a symbol of her hard work, dedication, and journey. Victor approached her, pride radiating from his every feature. "You did it, Lily. But remember, this is just the beginning. " Lily nodded, her heart swelling with gratitude and love—not just for tennis, but for life itself. The tournament was over, but the lessons learned echoed endlessly, rippling through her veins like an eternal game. She was ready to embrace everything that lay ahead, confident that she could face it all—with the fire ignited within her.

There sat Victor and Javier, their faces etched with unwavering support, pride radiating from their every expression like a lighthouse guiding her home through stormy seas. In their eyes, Lily found her anchor, a reminder that she was not alone in this moment. This, she realized, was more than just tennis; it was an intimate revelation about discovering her strength, her voice, and her will to fight against the odds. With that thought crystallizing in her mind, she anchored herself to the court ground beneath her and drew in a deep breath, feeling the cool air fill her lungs. The sounds of the world around her faded, becoming just a distant murmur—the whisper of the wind, the rustle of leaves, and the distant hum of spectators unaware of the battle unfolding deep within her heart. On the other side of the net stood an opponent, fierce and unapologetic. But in each bead of sweat on Lily's brow, she felt the weight of generations behind her. She thought of Victor, his quiet encouragement filling her when self-doubt threatened to sink its teeth into her resolve. And of Javier, whose laughter could lift her spirits even in the darkest of moments.

They were more than coaches; they were the embodiment of the lesson she was slowly learning: true strength is often found in vulnerability. She caught Victor's eye. In that brief exchange, a silent conversation passed between them—the certainty of a shared journey, the understanding that every point played was a testament to perseverance. She could almost hear Victor's voice, soft yet powerful, "Trust in yourself, Lily. You are stronger than you know." With that rhythm synchronizing with her heartbeat, she found clarity. Every puff of breath reminded her of the power she wielded—not just as a player, but as a warrior. Every swing of her racket began to echo with purpose, resonating through not just her body, but through her very soul. Each strike against the ball was not merely an act of competition; it became a declaration of her identity, each point fought a reclaiming of her narrative in a world that often tried to silence her. She could feel the energy of the court pulsing beneath her feet, and with every rally, she began to understand that tennis was a metaphor for life itself—a delicate dance of chaos and control, struggle and triumph.

The game taught her patience in defeat and humility in victory, but most importantly, it fostered resilience. Tennis, she realized, was more than a sport; it was a canvas on which she could paint her hopes, her dreams, her fears. The ball flew back and forth like the tides of a raging sea, but Lily was no longer adrift. She was learning to navigate those waters, to chart her own course, guided by the unwavering support of those who believed in her. As the match reached its crescendo, the stakes heightened, but so did her resolve. With each rally, she connected not just with the ball but with an inner strength that had been waiting to be unleashed. Her eyes flickered towards the stands once more, finding Victor and Javier. Their faith in her shone like a beacon, and in that moment, she became the embodiment of their lessons—bold, unyielding, and fiercely alive. In the end, whether she won or lost didn't matter. She could feel the transformation within her, illuminating the path that lay ahead—the lesson in life and tennis, a beautiful symphony of discovery and fortitude. And as she prepared to serve, she knew that the true victory was already hers.

In the quiet aftermath of the tournament, when the last echoes of applause for Lily faded, Victor found himself perched on the edge of the court. He exhaled slowly, watching the shadows grow longer, much like the memories of his career that danced before him. Victory danced just out of reach, a mirage shimmering in the distance. It mattered not if he left with a trophy that day. The true trophy lay in the quiet pride swelling within him. As he gazed out over the empty court, he was reminded of each serve, each rally, each victory and, yes, even the crushing defeats that had shaped his journey. Yet, it wasn't the trophies that defined him; it was the lives he had touched along the way. Turning to Javier—his most trusted confidant —Victor shared a thought that had settled deep in his heart. "Sometimes," he said, his voice barely above a whisper, "we find purpose not just in our triumphs, but in the lives we touch along the way." Javier nodded, understanding without the need for further explanation.

They had seen how the game transformed them, how it brought people together, each ball hit a heartbeat, each cheered a shared joy. The true essence of the game—and of life—unfurled before them like a well-worn racket, the strings frayed yet still resilient. "Remember that kid from the camp?" Javier continued, his mind drifting back to a summer long past. A boy named Sebastian, who had shuffled onto the court, knees shaking beneath his oversized shorts and too-big shoes. With every lesson learned, Javier had seen Sebastian transform from a timid player fearful of failure into a young man who stood tall, swinging fiercely at the ball. The last time they met, Sebastian had given Javier a small gift—the very bracelet he wore on his wrist, a token of gratitude. "It's a reminder," Sebastian told him, "that I can be strong just like you. "Javier felt a warmth spread through him, a reminder that victories could be measured not by the weight of a medal, but by the bonds forged in moments of shared struggle and triumph. Javier understood something profound: life, much like tennis, is not merely about winning. It's how you play the game. Every fault was a lesson, every match a chance to embrace one's vulnerabilities. Even amidst the competition, it was the love for the game—and for the people intertwined within it—that shone the brightest.

He and Victor stood together as the final rays of sunlight disappeared. "You know," Javier murmured, a smile creeping onto his face, "I am fully retiring, but it's not the end of my journey." He nudged Victor playfully, "I think I'll become a coach. Someone has to show others the beauty of this game." Victor chuckled, a twinkle of excitement in his eyes. "A coach with a heart, Javier? You'd be a legend." They shared a laugh, one that echoed through the empty courts—a reverberation of hope and joy that lingered just a little longer. As they walked away from the court, Javier felt lighter with each step. The echoes of their laughter whispered promises of what was to come. In that moment, he realized that the essence of life—and tennis—was not merely in the points won or lost, but in the connections made, the lessons learned, and the love shared along the way. With each sunset, new paths emerge.

The same could be said for his decision to coach; it marked the dawn of a new chapter. "Every ending is simply a new beginning," Javier thought, reflecting on years spent chasing victories. They were glorious; yet, there was a depth of richness in sharing that journey with others. He envisioned a group of young players gathering around him, eager eyes glistening with ambition. "Tennis is like life," he would say with passion filling his words, "both are not just about outcomes but also about growth." He imagined the stories he would share: the times he had lost, and how vulnerability had shaped his strength. He would teach them not only to swing their rackets but to embrace every moment—victories, defeats, and everything in between. Remembering his own journey, he felt the wounds of past losses still fresh; they reminded him that failure could become a stepping stone toward greatness. "It's in your fall that you gather strength," he would explain to his students. "Every missed shot is a chance to learn, every setback, a doorway to resilience." It was those lessons that transformed champions. Javier's hands would guide them through their triumphs and troubles, teaching them the voice of encouragement, and helping them find their own rhythm on and off the court. "Life isn't served on a silver platter," he would say, "it demands us to play with heart." Time passed, and seasons changed.

The quiet courts where Javier once played were teeming with vibrant energy. Youngsters laughed, practiced, and learned—each one holding onto the stories he shared. And in those moments, he understood that a legacy is not built on trophies but on the connections that transcend the game. As they stood together, facing the net, he shared another smile with Victor, who had become a faithful ally on this new journey. "See," he said, gesturing toward the eager faces, "this is my victory. Their smiles light up my heart." Victor nodded sagely, "You've proven that greatness is not defined by winning alone. In teaching, you've become a champion of life." As twilight descended, Javier looked back at the courts one last time. The canvases of his past melded with the colourful strokes of the new. "It's the final serve that matters most," he whispered, "the one that echoes in the hearts of the players we touch. " And so, he stepped forward—the sun had set on his playing career, but a new dawn awaited in the lives he would inspire.

With each player he coached, he served not just tennis balls but seeds of possibility, belief, and love. For in the heart of the game—and life—every serve could change a future, and every lesson could illuminate the path ahead. With renewed purpose, Javier embraced the light of the new chapter ahead. And, like a perfect rally, he knew life's greatest moments were never truly over; they simply continued to echo in the love shared along the way.

Epilogue.

As you embark on this remarkable journey of achievement, it is vital to recognize an undeniable truth: there will be no limits to what you can accomplish. This understanding isn't just an encouragement; it is a powerful affirmation of the potential that lies dormant within you, waiting to be awakened. Too often, we underestimate our capacity for greatness, allowing doubts and fears to cloud our vision of what is possible. Therefore, I urge you —never relinquish any task, nor allow the thought of any endeavour to fade simply because it appears daunting or beyond your reach. Let us draw inspiration from nature, specifically from the tenacious snowdrop shoot that bravely emerges from the unforgiving earth. Imagine this delicate yet determined plant, pushing its way through layers of frost and grime.

Its existence is a testament to resilience and inner spirit. What courage it takes to break through the stubborn ground, especially when the outcome is uncertain! There is no guarantee that once it reaches the surface, it will be greeted warmly by sunlight or nurtured by the accommodating earth. Consider the adversity this small shoot encounters—the cold, the darkness, the weight of the soil above it. In your own life, you may face obstacles that seem insurmountable, challenges that make you question your abilities and motivations. It is easy to succumb to the belief that certain goals are unattainable, that dreams are too lofty. But like the snowdrop, you possess an inherent drive—a powerful urge that compels you to pursue your aspirations, no matter how formidable the task may seem. This inner urge, represented by the small seed buried deep within the earth, serves as a reminder of your true nature. Just as the snowdrop is genetically coded to rise, flourish, and reveal its beauty, so too are you designed to achieve.

The very essence of existence is progress and evolution. Your journey may be fraught with setbacks and hardships, but within those challenges lies the seed of potential—if you only nurture it with determination and belief. Embrace the discomfort of growth. It is through struggle that strength is forged. The snowdrop doesn't give up when the task feels insurmountable; it perseveres, driven by an innate force to live, to thrive, to share its beauty with the world. You, too, must engage with that inner voice that whispers, "Keep going!" Beyond every obstacle lies an opportunity for growth and transformation. When doubts creep in, ask yourself: what is it that holds you back? Often, it is the fear of failure or the unease of stepping outside your comfort zone. But consider this: the true failure lies not in falling short of your goals, but in never having the courage to try. By entertaining the prospect of failure, you curtail your potential. Allow yourself to take risks, to venture into the unknown, to rise against the odds like a resilient snowdrop. So, as you stand at the precipice of your aspirations, I urge you to embrace the challenges ahead. Nurture that seed within yourself, cultivate your tenacity, and remember that every great accomplishment begins with the decision to try. The world is waiting for you to blossom into your fullest self, to reveal the beauty and strength that resides within you. The path may not always be easy, but it is yours to light. Trust in your ability to navigate the uncharted waters of your potential. Lift your gaze, take a deep breath, and press on boldly toward your dreams. The sky is not just the limit; it is merely the beginning.

About the Author.

James Corden-Lloyd, a PTR Performance Coach, TEFL Teacher and Author. He employs a distinctive method that utilizes the physical and social aspects of tennis to foster an engaging language learning atmosphere, specifically designed for those learning English as a Second Language (ESL). He is the founder of Corden Tennis and English Academy.

Printed in Dunstable, United Kingdom